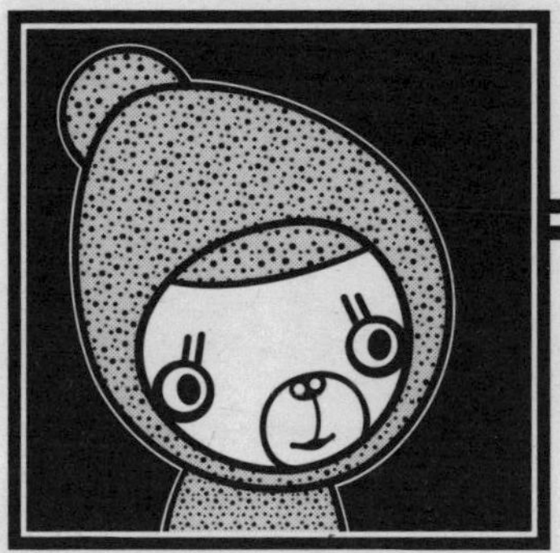

How drawing changed the world Edited by Gordon Shrigley

Published by marmalade
© marmalade 2004
Individual chapters
© contributors

ISBN 0–9546597–0–8

Designed by Daniel Welton
of www.eightdesign.com
Cover drawing
© Gordon Shrigley

Set in 9 on 11.25pt,
Univers 45 and 65

Printed and bound in
Great Britain by Bookmarque
Ltd, Croydon, Surrey

www.marmalade@inter.uk.com

spatula

Contents

Imagine, it is the 5th of September 1977 and you are standing in the noonday sun in Cape Canaveral, Florida watching a small spacecraft hurtle up into the blue majestic sky above you to begin a journey into the cosmic unknown far, far, far away. Attached to the side of this small craft, which is no larger than a domestic washing machine, is fixed a 12–inch gold-plated copper phonograph record, wrapped in a protective aluminium foil. Upon this disc, diligently collected by the leading scientists of the day, are a small sample of sounds and images, recorded in anologue form, to portray the incredible diversity and culture of the history of humanity to any curious alien DJ, still collecting records.

How did the designers of this highly collectable record choose to communicate with beings, who we can be assured have had a very different cultural history to our own? The medium they chose was drawing. For upon the cover of this spinning ambassador for humanity were drawn a series of line diagrams, designed to communicate to anyone or anything coming across this piece of space junk, instructions of how to spin this record. So enabling this peculiarly foreign listener to discover within the very lines inscribed upon the records surface, a video stream of the salient features of humanity as told through a series of mathematical equations, documentary photographs, diagrams and anatomical cartoons.

Was drawing the only means available to communicate our distinctive human qualities to a passing alien? What is so special about the graphic line, that is adequate to this Herculean task of description? Here is a short excerpt from a text published by NASA at the time, to describe how their intergalactic instruction manual (the *World Book*) was to work:

'The top drawing shows the typical signal that occurs at the start of a picture. The picture is made from this signal, which traces the picture as a series of vertical lines, similar to ordinary television (in which the picture is a series of horizontal lines). Picture lines 1, 2, and 3 are noted in binary numbers, and the duration of one of the 'picture lines,' about 8 milliseconds, is noted. The drawing immediately below shows how these lines are to be drawn vertically, with staggered 'interlace' to give the correct picture rendition. Immediately below this is a drawing of an entire picture raster, showing there are 512 vertical lines in a complete picture.'[1]

1

Passage taken from the National Aeronautics Space Agency, Jet Propulsion laboratory, California Institute of Technology website: www.jpl.nasa.gov/index.html

Perhaps Carl Sagan, the then chairman of the selection committee for the *World Book*, who went on to host the globally syndicated *Cosmos* television series, and his fellow researchers did not stop to think twice about employing the graphic line as a super-transcendent form of communication. For perhaps it was clearly evident to them as it still is, for us today, that line is the pre-eminent mode of communication shared by all human beings and any hapless space traveller unlucky enough to land on our shores would quickly conclude that humans are primarily extremely inventive line workers.

I guess this statement may appear a little contentious, but just stop for one moment and consider that if I were to ask you to draw up a complete list of all the things that have been designed through drawing which form part of your everyday life; your car, house, sofa, computer, mobile phone, hi-fi, credit card, bicycle, refrigerator, video camera, clothes, trainers, cooker, dining table, kettle, ironing board, books, toothbrush… how long this list would really have to be? As nearly everything we produce in the modern world, has been in one form or another, drawn and projected first through the graphic line.[2]

The language that you and I speak, write and think with, is also another example of the many linear phonetic alphabets that have been invented over time in the form of letters, words and finally perhaps literature.[3] In this sense, our patent desire for mark-making, translates into one of the central ways we reason as conscious beings. Which by dividing the world into ever more complex distinctions between phenomena, has over the centuries of human exploration effectively recreated the world as one vast linear diagram.

[2]
For a detailed description of the history and practice of descriptive drawing see: Fred Dubery and John Willats, *Drawing Systems*, Studio Vista, 1972 and Thomas E French and Carl L Svensen, *Mechanical Drawing*, McGraw-Hill Book Company, 1957

[3]
The earliest phonetic alphabet, Vinca, dates from between the 7th–4th millennia BC and has been found on artefacts excavated in Greece, Bulgaria, Romania, eastern Hungary, Moldova, southern Ukraine and former Yugoslavia and remains undeciphered. For an extensive description of ancient writing systems visit the Omniglot website: www.omniglot.com/index.htm

Admittedly this is a partisan view, but is it not tempting to see the entire history of humanity as one epic story of how we have played with and thought through line? Whether that be by painting on a cave wall to record heroic exploits or the measured discipline required to design and build a spacecraft, the drawing of lines is the one unifying activity which links both of these very singular practices.

What is a line? What possibilities does line offer? Is line really a simple tool or does our addiction to drawing and thinking through line, structure the way we see the world in any way?

To start to answer these questions we have invited artists and writers to discuss through words and images how line effects the practice and thinking of their subjects. Depending on who is doing the talking of course, line may be made to signify any number of different material and conceptual processes. Accordingly *Spatula* has been designed to provide the reader with an extensive range of examples of talking through line, from the deadpan world of science to the carefree irreverence of the cartoon.

Not quite a dictionary of line or a theoretical treatise, *Spatula* mixes the genres of the comic, the journal and the learned essay so as to begin to understand how drawing changed the world.

Lines, the way I understand and use them, are a language. Lines are devices which help me to express my thoughts and emotions, and so, for me, lines are not simple tools that are to be rendered invisible at the culmination of the work. On the contrary, lines play an important part within my visual stories. It is what there is to see, along with surfaces, colours… and in fact, to separate all these elements does not help to come any closer to a specific story. A line can also easily become a surface or a colour – it all depends on the surroundings.

Starting with an idea for a story, I search through photographs, drawings, paintings, data that belong to such various fields as biology, arts, personal memories, politics… and also produce, shoot or draw specific things. The motifs I choose are then caught by tracing them with a few lines that are simple and without expressive gesture. This partial going over with line releases the motif from its entanglements, allowing it to be placed in a constellation of motifs, free from their different thematic origins.

The traced motifs can be seen as protagonists, that now enter into a play that is concentrated on relations of spaces within, around and between them. This is an exciting and surprising part of developing a story. Moving the elements, using different techniques to provoke tactile sensations, to introduce density, deepness and distances… it is a way of furnishing an imaginary new world. During this process, I use these nuances and constellations to play with the tension of the emotional whole. The finished story is stored as data and is finally exposed on photographic paper. The size of the image is an important part of this work. Viewing the work on a small scale, for example say in a documentation, can guide us to focus on naming things. But seeing an image with a height of 120 cm, allows us to see the varied nuances of texture, colour, form and space and thereby lets us concentrate on the tension and possible relations between them.

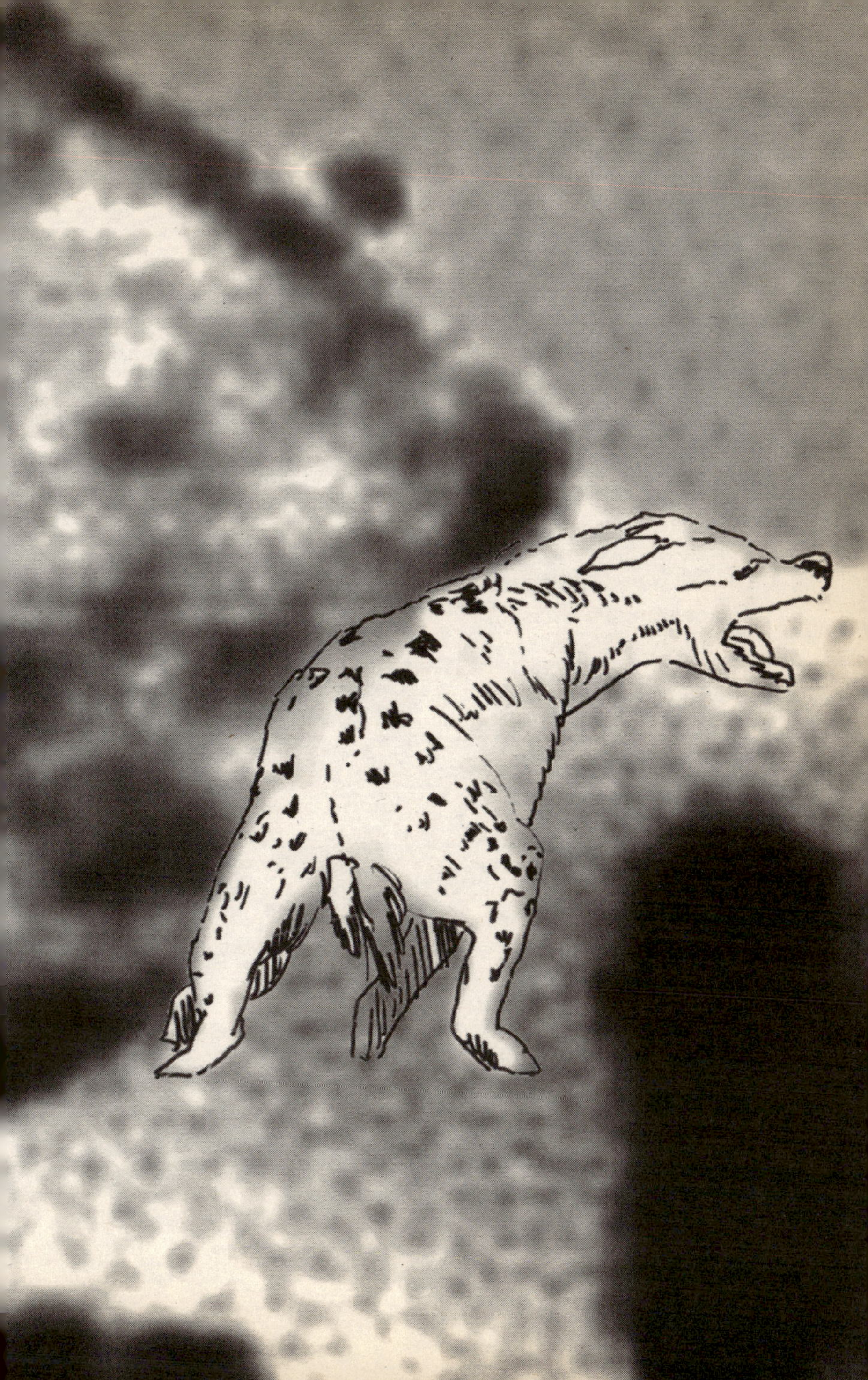

The carpet of life

The carpet of life

lines turn into evil
spinked mountains

and elegant voracious hyenas

circumscribe
gardens full of
blossoming flowers

divide forests
from shallow ponds

structure open vast
planes

and brake
through even skies

Like stepping stones laid in moss in a Japanese garden,
that slow the spectator's pace and satisfy the need for calm,
drawn stories invite us to emotionally relax and be mentally
active. We can contemplate on what we see, leaving the
rigid social hierarchies of the everyday world behind us. In
our imagination, we can play out different possibilities that
the narrative could take. We are offered an intensive world
that lies open for discovery and rethinking of one's own
experiences that can alter one's position towards it and
lead to new outlooks.

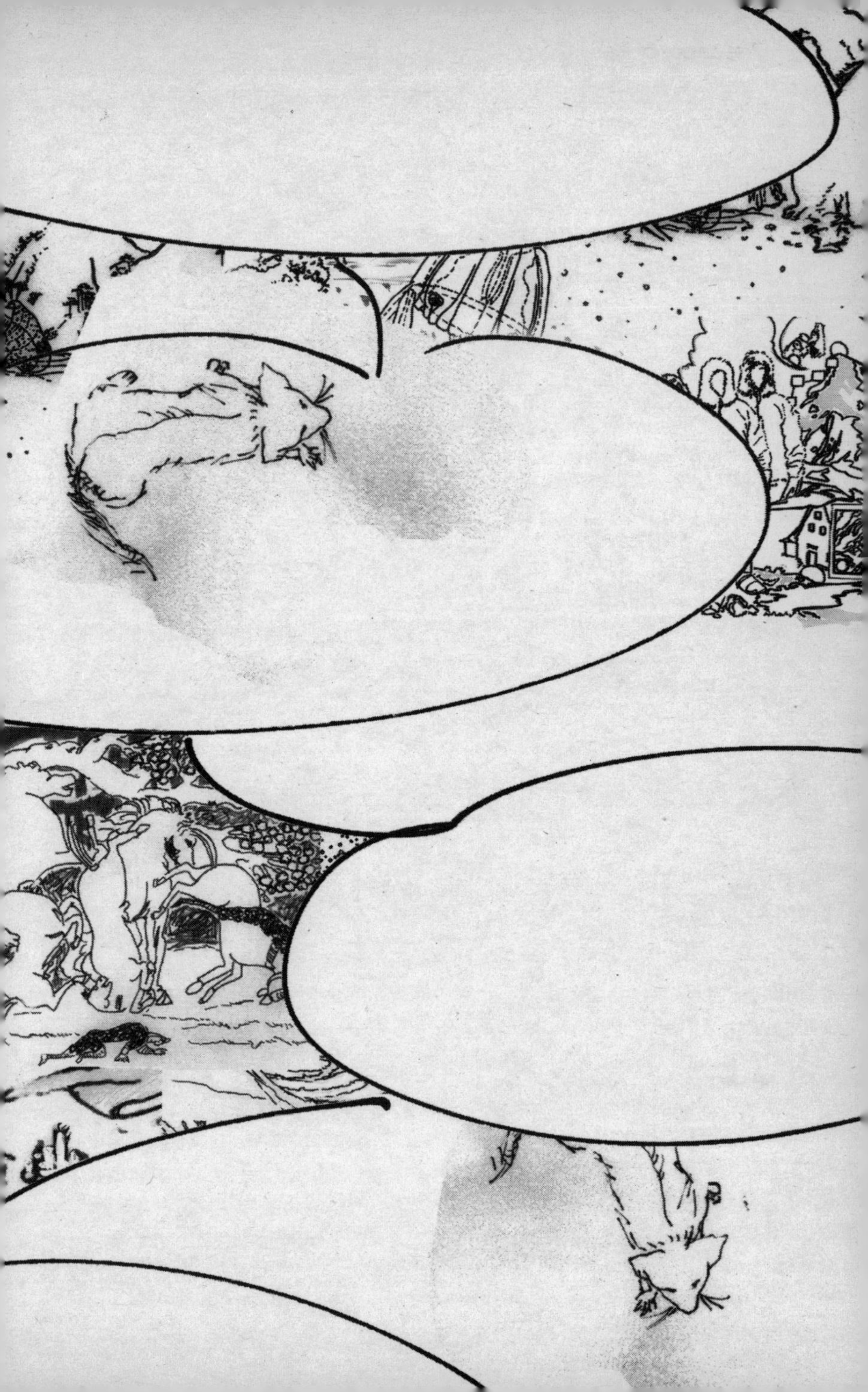

The carpet of life

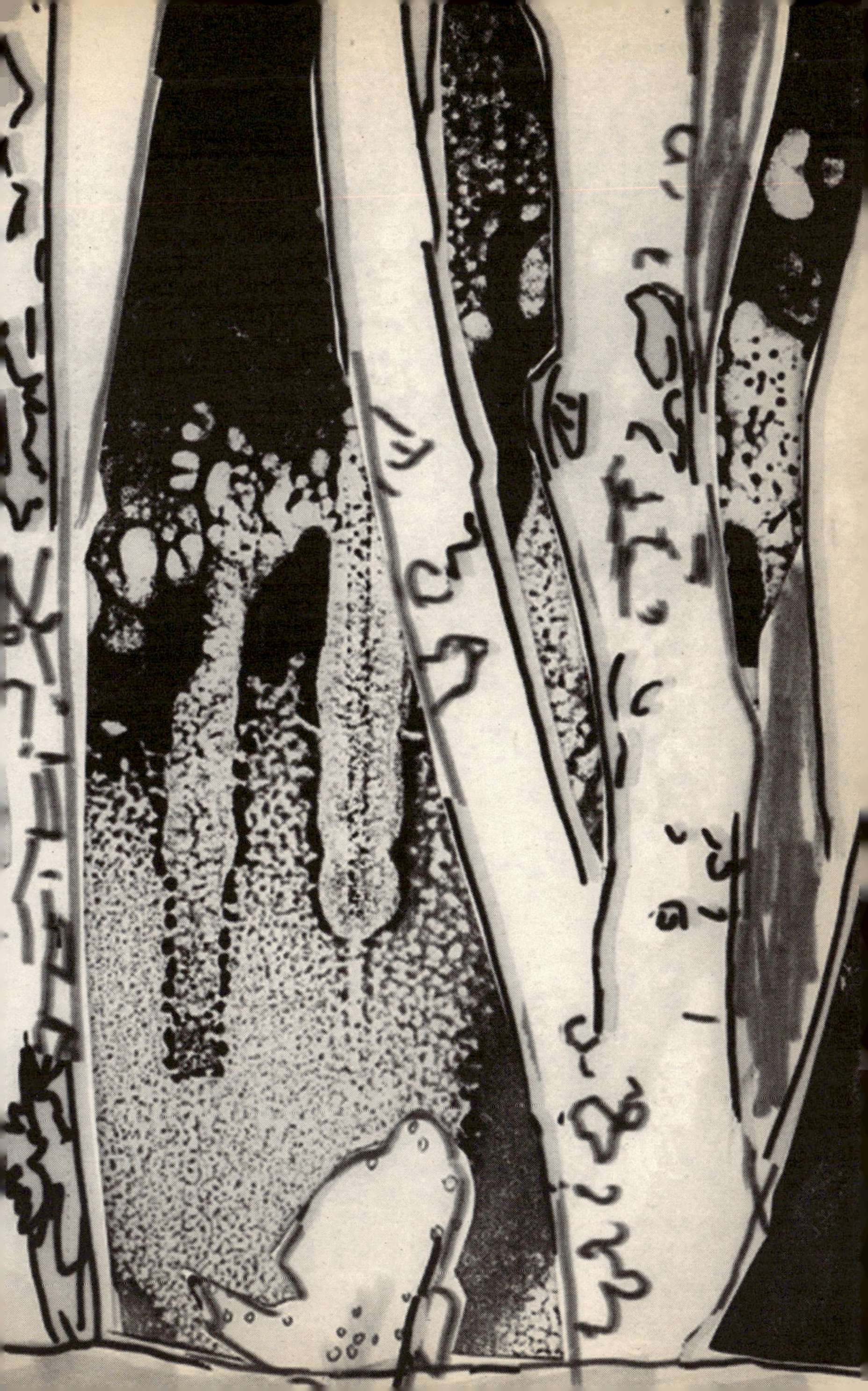

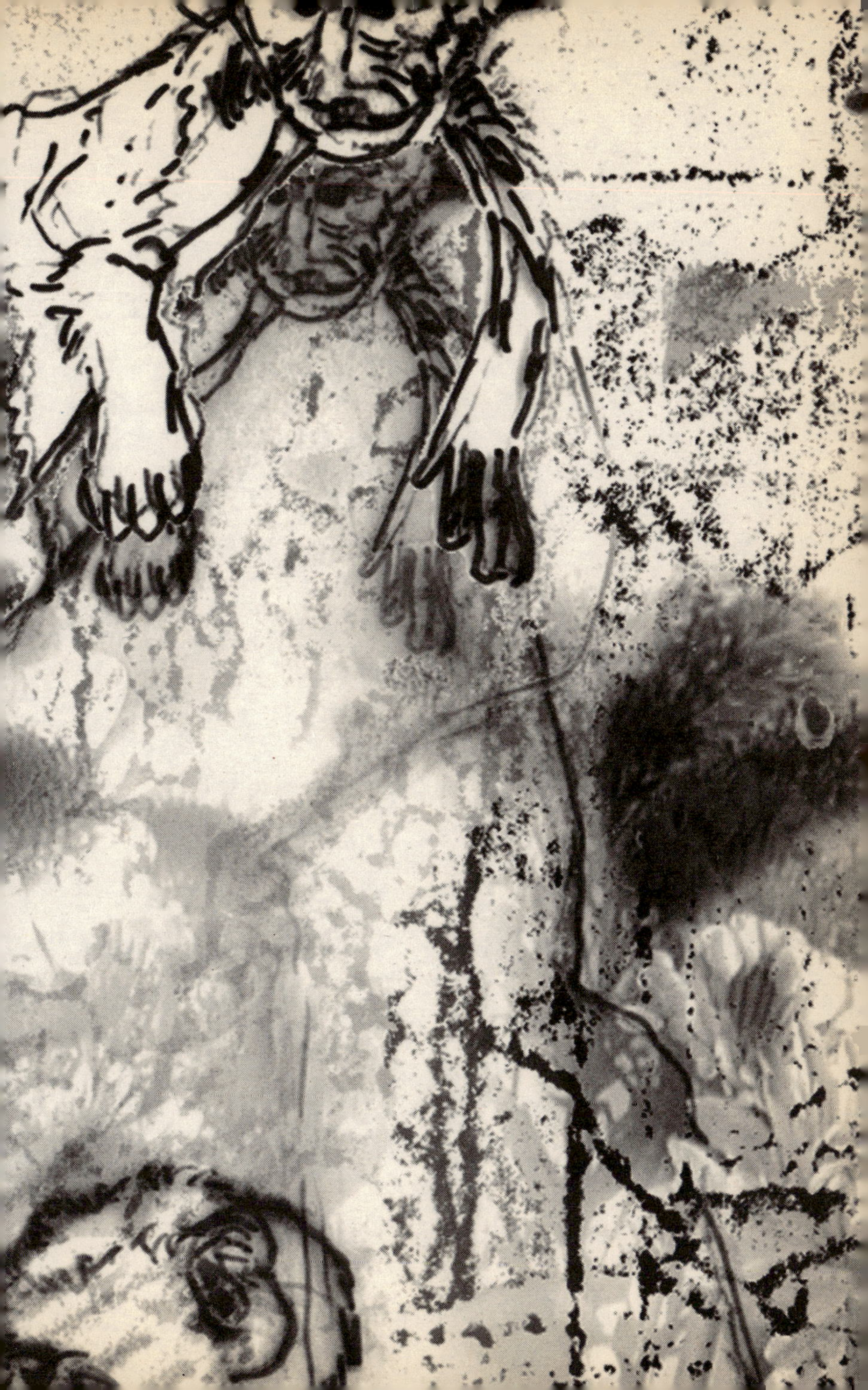

Simple things

For those with an interest in the most fundamental components of reality, reflecting on the simplest of things can yield a rich harvest. Consider two buttons, of exactly the same shade of red, one round and made of plastic, the other square and made of wood. Each button is clearly a distinct object in its own right: each is composed of a different portion of matter, each has its own spatial location. But are the buttons completely distinct? It might seem so, but a little reflection can suggest otherwise.

Both buttons are the same colour, they are each red. The buttons do not possess merely *similar* colours, they possess literally *identical* colours: one and the same colour, a particular shade of red, is found in both objects. This same colour can also be found in many other objects. Colour, it seems, is not tied down to any specific time or place, in the way ordinary objects are. The same (literally identical) colour can exist at many times and places. And what holds for colour also holds for other common characteristics, such as shapes and sizes, and sounds. We are thus led to the (now familiar) distinction between *particulars* (spatially located objects) and *universals* (repeatable, multiple located properties).

Plato was no stranger to this line of reasoning, but he found himself driven to take several further steps. He observed that in ordinary life we never encounter a truly perfect circle (or square, or triangle, or straight line), but that we nonetheless have the concept of such a circle. Relying on the (by no means absurd) assumption that meaningful terms must have referents – in order to be meaningful at all – he was led to the conclusion that the perfect circle must exist in a non-physical plane of reality, a dimension where perfection is possible. He called this changeless, timeless realm the world of Forms. He further reasoned that since a circle is a universal, all other universals (such as redness) must inhabit this realm also. Resemblances among the familiar objects in the physical world are to be explained in terms of Forms participating, more or less adequately, in these objects.

The theory also had epistemological implications. If we never encounter a perfect circle (or straight line, or triangle) in the physical world, how is it that we possess the concept of one? Plato drew the (seemingly) obvious conclusion: since we cannot acquire such concepts from observation, we must possess them innately. Where does this innate knowledge originate? Where else than the realm of Forms. But how can we have knowledge of the realm of Forms? There must be a part of us – a non-physical part, a soul – that has an affinity with this realm, and hence access to it.

There are not many, these days, who are prepared to follow Plato all the way. But, needless to say, there is little consensus on where and exactly how his reasoning is flawed, and much ink has been spilled on the topic down the centuries. For present purposes, the details of this debate matter less than the more general lessons that can be drawn from it. First, Plato's argument constitutes a prime example of how reflecting on the simplest of things – coloured objects, a line drawn in the sand – can yield a harvest that is rich, but also mixed. Genuine and enduring insights are closely intermingled with errors and false trails. Plato's highly influential reflections advanced our understanding, but also obstructed our progress. Second, and more specifically, reflecting on the nature of line can be a fertile source of both insight and confusion.

In what follows I will consider some further ways in which our intuitive understanding of the nature of line and linearity have exerted an influence on how we conceive of reality in general. My principle topic is not resemblance, but something of similarly fundamental importance: the nature of space and time.

Space

The world we encounter in everyday experience consists of objects spread through and separated by space. What sort of thing is this space with which we are all so familiar? The very question can seem misguided. It only makes sense to ask what *sort* of thing space is if space is a *thing*. But isn't it clear that space is *not* a thing of any kind? We are told that the galaxies are separated by vast tracts of empty space. What distinguishes all this empty space from nothingness pure and simple? The answer might seem plain: absolutely nothing. The idea that space is simply nothingness, a void in the strictest and most literal sense, is confirmed by more mundane considerations. We can make sense of a machine which sucks out everything from a room – ie, all matter, all air particles, all energy and radiation – but could there be a machine which sucked *space* out from a room? The notion seems absurd. When everything has been removed from a room, nothing whatsoever remains, and this nothing is simply empty space.

The doctrine that space is indistinguishable from nothingness – the Void Conception as we can call it – has considerable intuitive appeal, but further reflection reveals it to be untenable. Whatever its nature, our space performs two roles that a void-space is manifestly unable to perform: it *connects* and *constrains*.

The connecting role of space is obvious. To simplify, let us suppose every object in our universe is annihilated, save for two distant planets. The scenario is eminently imaginable, and immediately reveals a difficulty for the Void Conception. The two planets that remain are distant, which entails that they are also at some *distance from* one another. Whatever distance may involve, it involves at least this: objects separated by some distance are *connected* in a distinctive way – they are connected in a way objects in different universes (different, unconnected spaces) can never be. By equating space with absolute nothingness, the Void Conception fails to accommodate or explain the fact that objects existing in the same space are separated by specific distances.

The constraining role of space is equally real, but rather more elusive. Why is it that we can only move in three dimensions? The question seems odd: up–down, left–right, forward–back, and all directions in-between – what other directions could there be? But reflect for a moment on the predicament of the point-like inhabitants of one-dimensional Lineland.[1] There is no reason for the Linelanders to feel constrained, to suppose there are directions other than back and forth. Nothing in their everyday experience suggests that their universe is other than one-dimensional, and evolution – with its usual parsimony – has not equipped them with the ability to imagine and visualize in more than one dimension. That there are other directions in which motion is possible seems obvious to us, but this is because we actually inhabit a three-dimensional space – we *know* there are other directions. However, the idea that there are, or could be, many dimensions beyond the three with which we are familiar, will – on first encountering it, at least – strike most of us as bizarre in the extreme. But from a purely mathematical perspective, a four-, five- or *n*-dimensional space is just as possible as a three-dimensional space. Logically speaking, it is perfectly possible for there to be five-dimensional beings who are able to look down on our three-dimensional space in just the way we look down on the Linelanders. It would be just as obvious to these beings that there are directions beyond our knowledge and comprehension as it is obvious to us that there are directions beyond the comprehension of the Linelanders.

So, a question has to be addressed: given the logical possibility of spaces with more than three dimensions, why is it that, in actual fact, we are confined to moving in three dimensions? What explains this constraint? One thing is clear. If the Void Conception were true, there would be no reason whatsoever why we should be constrained in the ways we are.

---

[1] Figure 3 depicts one possible Lineland (of a rather uneven sort). For further explorations of lower (and higher) dimensional spaces see Edwin A Abbot, *Flatland: A Romance of many Dimensions by a Square*, New York: Penguin, 1986 and Iain Stewart, *Flatterland*, London: Macmillan, 2001

There are two solutions to the connection and constraint problems, the merits of which continue to be debated. One option is to reject void-space in favour of substantival space. Substantivalists view space as a three-dimensional homogeneous medium, a spatial *substance*, as it were. The relationship of material objects to this medium is (roughly) analogous to that of a fish to water (see figure 1). The distances and direction in which a fish can swim are determined by the body of water in which it finds itself; in like fashion, the ways material bodies can move are determined by the shape, size and dimensionality of the spatial medium in which they find themselves. On this view, distances are paths through substantival space, and it only makes sense to claim that two objects are at a certain distance from one another if both exist in the same spatial substance.

Conceiving of space as substantival may solve the connection and constraint problems, but – in the eyes of many – it introduces a new and serious problem of its own. If space is substance-like, it is a substance of a peculiar sort. Not only is it invisible to the eye, it offers not the least resistance to bodies which move through it. What differentiates such an ethereal substance from nothingness? Shouldn't a genuine substance have discernible properties in its own right?

Considerations such as these inspired the competing *relational* conception of space. The basic idea is simple. We dispense with the substantival space, and replace it with a network of relations between material objects, which we can conceive as being composed of point-particles existing in void-space. The relations are of a distinctive sort: *distance-*relations. A distance-relation is akin to a perfectly straight line of force linking objects, one that is indefinitely extendible and contractible (objects can move further apart and closer together), and it is invisible and intangible (we cannot see or touch distance-relations). As well as connecting objects, distance-relations also constrain them: the dimensionality of a universe is determined by the (law-governed) orientations distance-relations can adopt relative to one another.[2]

2

See a more detailed account of different conceptions of space through the ages, see Max Jammer, *Concepts of Space* (3rd edition), London: Dover, 1993

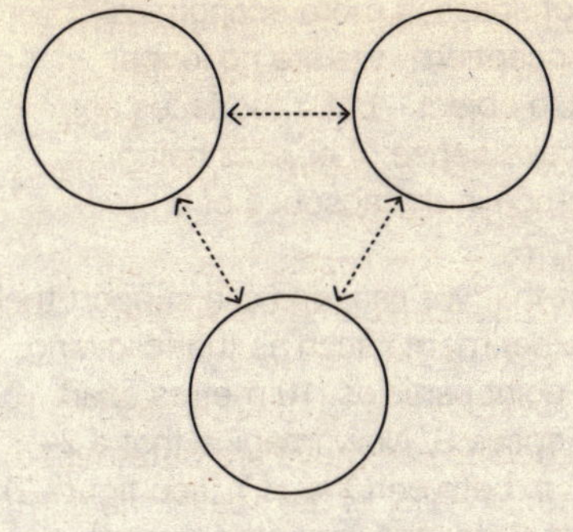

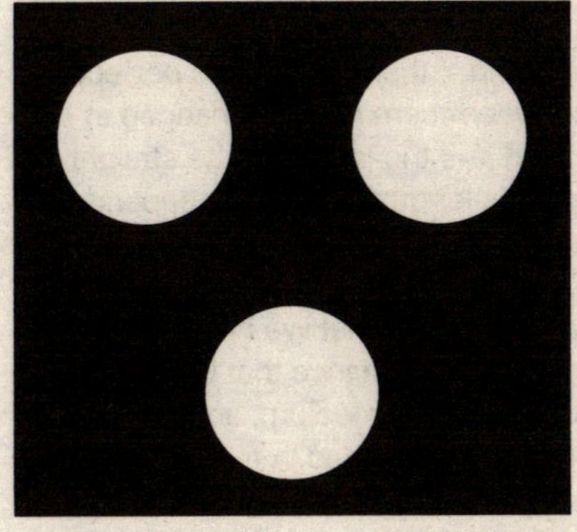

Figure 1
Competing
conceptions of space:
relationalism and
substantivalism

The relational conception of space is more economical than the substantivalist conception – we are no longer positing a vast unobservable object – but it too faces an objection. Can we really make sense of objects being connected by lines of distance in the absence of a surrounding spatial medium?

Relationalists insist that we can, and can support their contention with thought-experiments such as the following. Suppose X and Y are two point-particles, 10 metres apart, embedded in substantival space S. Now imagine that a 2–metre hole is created in S, in between X and Y (see figure 2). Since for the substantivalist distances are paths through a spatial substance, the creation of the hole in S has increased the distance between X and Y, since the shortest connecting path through S is longer than it was. But the relationalist will insist that if we focus on X and Y themselves, it is perfectly clear that the distance between them has not changed at all. The distance between X and Y is the length of the straight line connecting them, and this length is entirely independent of the presence (or absence) of *anything* else, putative substantival space included.[3]

Examples such as this reveal that we have an intuitive conception of straight-line distance that is entirely independent of a surrounding spatial medium, and the relational conception of space is grounded in this conception. However, it is by no means clear that anything in reality – as opposed to our imaginings – corresponds with this conception, and it is even less clear that distance-relations, thus conceived, could be sufficient to bind the physical universe into a spatially unified whole. Substantivalists maintain they could not, and so conclude that our intuitive conception of straight-line distance has been a hindrance in our attempts to understand the nature of physical space, rather than revelatory of its real nature.[4]

[3]
See P Bricker, 'The Fabric of Space, Midwest Studies', in, *Philosophy XVIII*, (ed.) French, Uehling, Notre Dame, Wettstein: Notre Dame University Press, 1993

[4]
See also Graham Nerlich, *The Shape of Space*, Cambridge: CUP, 1994, chapter 1. I have been concentrating here on the metaphysical aspect of relationalism. For more on this topic see Julian Barbour, *Absolute and Relative Motion*, Cambridge: CUP, 1999 and *The End of Time*, London: Weidenfeld and Nicholson, 1993, Lawrence Sklar, *Space, Time and Spacetime*, Berkeley: University of California Press, 1975, J Earman *World Enough and Spacetime*, Cambridge: MIT, 1989 and Dainton *Time and Space*, Chesham: Acumen, 2001, chapters 9–14

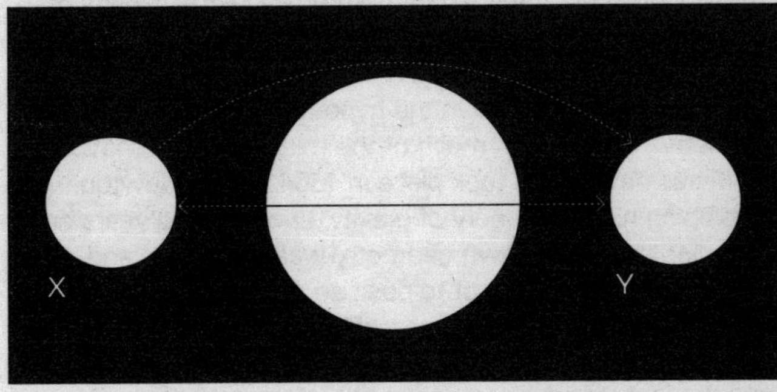

Figure 2
Competing intuitions:
does the creation of
a hole in the two-
dimensional space
shown above affect
the distance between
X and Y?

There is another reason for supposing this to be the case, one we have not yet considered.

Although the debate between substantivalism and relationism is as yet unresolved, most would agree that our current best theory of the large-scale universe, Einstein's general theory of relativity (GTR), is most naturally construed as positing a substantival spatiotemporal medium. The space-time of GTR is also of variable curvature: the precise geometry of space-time is influenced by the distribution of mass-energy; gravitational effects are the product of space-time curvature – freely falling objects follow geodesic (straightest path) trajectories. In formulating GTR, Einstein relied upon the extant mathematical treatments of curved spaces. These had been developed only a few years earlier: Einstein completed GTR in 1915, Riemann's groundbreaking lecture 'On the hypotheses which underlie geometry', from which much of the relevant mathematical work was developed, took place in 1854. When Newton was developing his own theory of gravity, two hundred years or so earlier, the only known geometry was Euclidean, and so Newton had no option but to posit an action-at-a-distance force, a force which Einstein revealed to be redundant. That no serious work was done on the geometry of curved spaces until the eighteenth and ninetheenth centuries is in many respects puzzling. Geometry was the earliest branch of mathematics to reach maturity; the thirteen books of Euclid's Elements were completed in 300BC. Why did it take another two thousand years for geometers to move decisively beyond Euclid?

The unrivalled brilliance of the Elements themselves is in part responsible: it was far from obvious that further work in the field remained to be done. But there is a deeper explanation. In order to take seriously the idea that a curved manifold (not necessarily two-dimensional) could be a *space* it is necessary to move beyond our intuitive understanding of what constitutes a straight line. A straight line is defined as the shortest possible distance between two points. In two-dimensional sphere-geometry, where space is construed as

being constituted by the *surface* of a sphere, the shortest
distance between two points will lie on the great circles
(or circumferences) connecting the points on the sphere's
surface. Evidently, it is not easy to accept that curved lines
such as these can be *straight* – surely, we naturally think, the
truly straight lines, the real paths of shortest distance, are
those all too easily imaginable connecting lines which take
the short-cut *through* the sphere, not the longer curves which
cling to its surface. In like fashion, it is hard to believe that a
curved line in a three-dimensional space could ever be the
shortest distance between two points lying in such a space.
For whatever curved path we consider, we can always
imagine, easily imagine, a truly straight line, one that is
shorter in length, connecting the points in question.
Consequently, the idea that a curved line could be the
shortest distance (and so the straightest line) between
two locations in our space can easily seem ridiculous.

But such reactions, while natural, are also misguided.
To return to the two-dimensional case, if we take the surface
of a sphere to *be* a space, then all possible spatial paths –
all possible lines – lie on the sphere-surface; the easily
envisaged lines cutting through the sphere do not and cannot
exist in this space. And the same applies to the supposed
truly straight lines cutting through a curved three-dimensional
space (or one-dimensional space, see figure 3). To insist that
such lines *do* in fact exist is simply to beg the question
against the possibility of non-Euclidean spaces.

This is a simple point, no doubt, but only with the
benefit of hindsight. The intuitive notion which the straight
line exerts has such compelling power that generations of
the most gifted mathematicians failed to grasp the point in
question. And our understanding of space – of the possible
ways a space can be has long suffered accordingly.

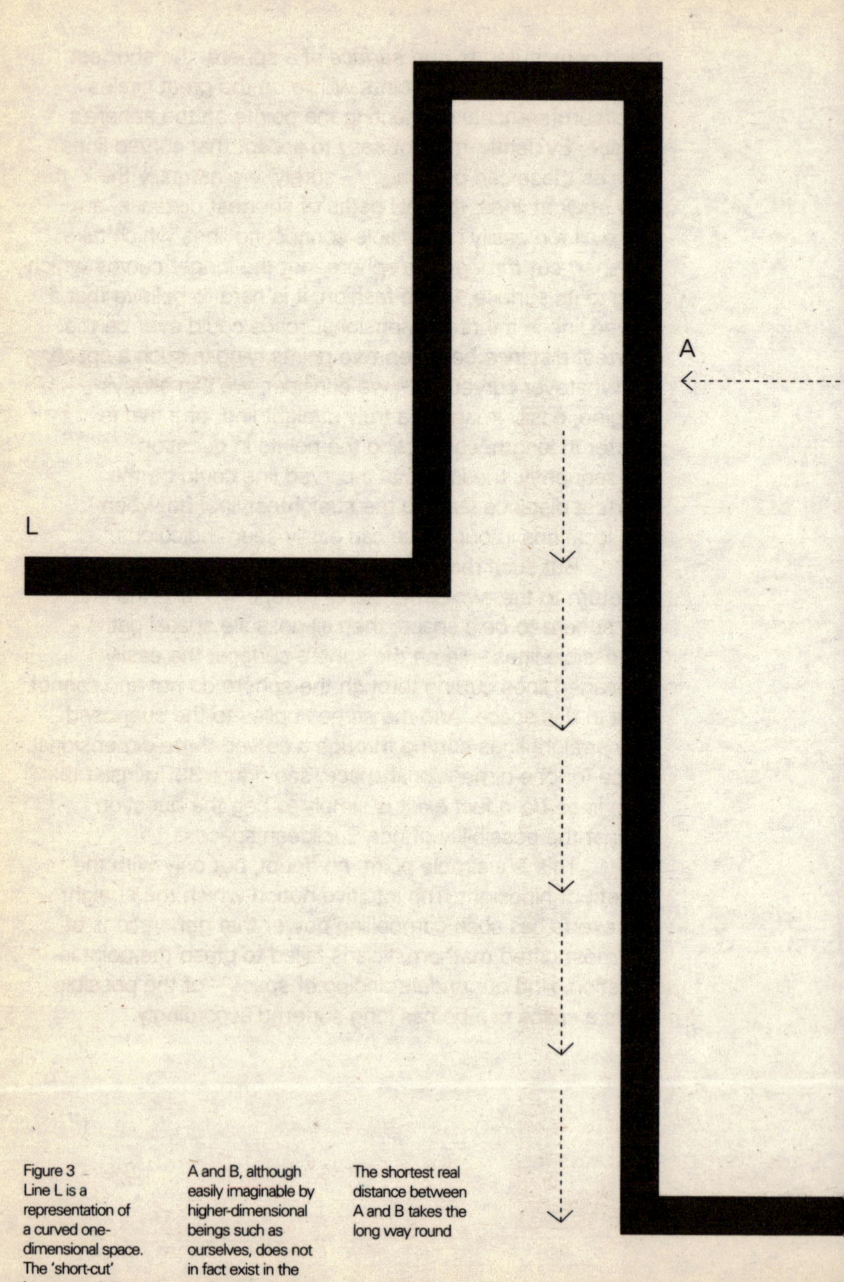

Figure 3
Line L is a
representation of
a curved one-
dimensional space.
The 'short-cut'
between points

A and B, although
easily imaginable by
higher-dimensional
beings such as
ourselves, does not
in fact exist in the
envisaged universe.

The shortest real
distance between
A and B takes the
long way round

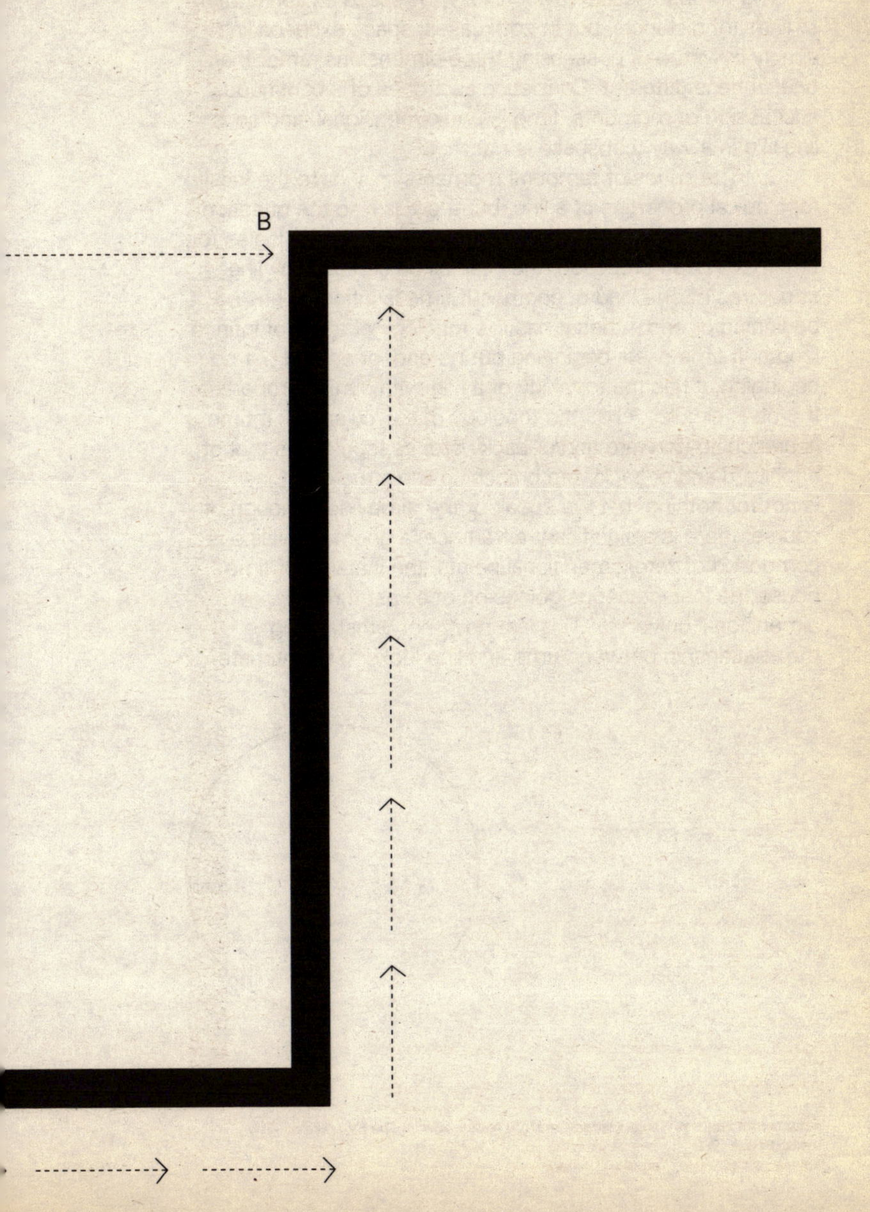

B

Time

The relationship between line and time is more direct than between line and space. Substantivalists view lines as passing *through* space, relationists view space as constituted *of* lines (of distance), but in both cases, space exceeds line simply by virtue of possessing three-dimensions rather than one. Time is different. Consisting as it does of a continuous succession of moments, time is one-dimensional, and so is line-like in a way that space is not.

The series of temporal moments may have the local topological properties of a line, but there is also the question of *global* topology. But although different global topologies for time have been proposed, they can all be captured by line-structures of one kind or another. If time is infinite – has no beginning or end – then it has the topology of a line of infinite length; if time has a beginning but no end, or an end but no beginning, it has the topology of a line with similar properties. If time is circular, it has the topology of a circular line; if time is branching (forward and/or backward) its topology is that of a forward and/or backward branching line-structure. Clearly, it is not for nothing that we speak of the 'time-line'. Though of course, there is a significant difference: a geometrical line is composed of zero-dimensional points, the instants of time house the instantaneous goings-on of a vast three-dimensional universe.[5] This last point notwithstanding, the relationship between time and line looks to be intimate.

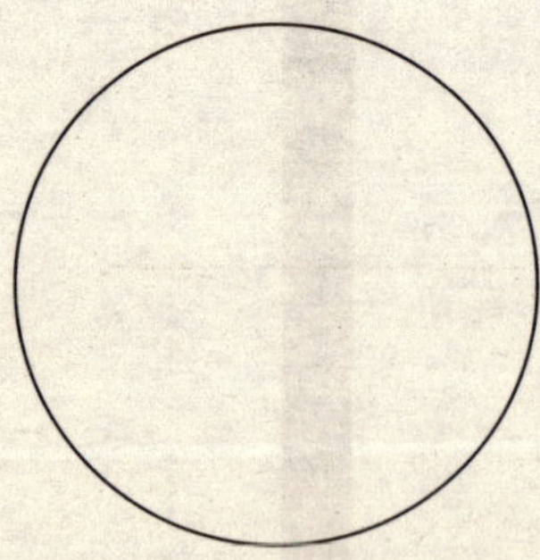

5
For more on these structural matters, see WH Newton-Smith, *The Structure of Time*, London: RKP, 1980

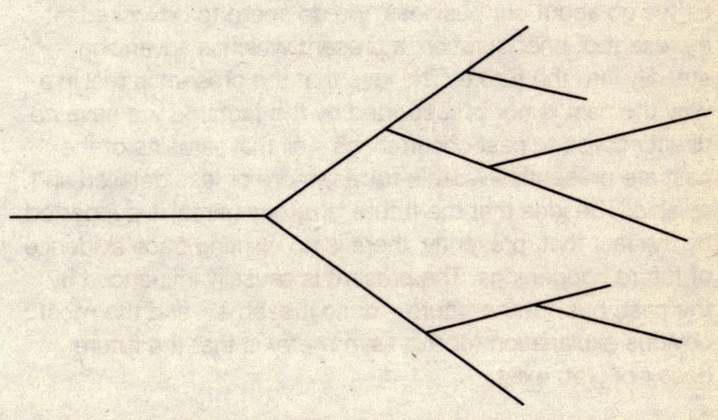

Figure 4
Three temporal
topologies: circular,
linear and branching

However, viewed in another way, time is *less* like line than space. There may be a dimensional difference between line and physical space, but this numerical difference is overshadowed by an equivalence on the ontological level. A line consists of a series of points, all of which have exactly the same ontological status: all are equally real. The points in three-dimensional (substantival) physical space share this feature: all are equally real. Time seems different; it is surely more than a static ensemble of locations, we are inclined to think, for the simple reason that *time* passes, whereas space does not. At the very least, the passage of time involves the steady movement of the present into the future. There is no spatial counterpart of a moving present in a purely spatial dimension. It is also natural to suppose that temporal passage has ontological implications. Many of us believe that present happenings are real in a way past happenings are not; still more of us are inclined to believe that whereas present happenings are undeniably real, the future has no reality whatsoever – future events *will* be real, but only when the present has advanced that far. Again, there is no spatial counterpart of these ontological differences: the places to the north of here are just as real as those to the south.

There are different ways of fleshing out the dynamic conception of time, but the central contention, that we inhabit a moving, privileged present, has enormous appeal. After all, as we go about our business, we do seem to be locked into a present of brief duration, a present which is advancing steadily into the future. The idea that the present is real in a way the past is not is supported by the fact that we have no direct access to past occurrences – all that remains of the past are presently available traces, more or less detailed and reliable. The idea that the future is utterly unreal is supported by the fact that, presently, there is no existing trace-evidence of future happenings. The present is causally influenced by the past, but not the future – or so it seems – and the most obvious explanation for this asymmetry is that the future does not (yet) exist.

Dynamic conceptions of time may have intuitive appeal, but it has proved curiously difficult to formulate detailed dynamic accounts which are free of obvious flaws. To note just one central problem: how are we to make sense of the idea that the present *moves*? If we say that the present is located in 1900, then in 1901, then in 1902, etc, we seem to be postulating a state of affairs in which our time-line endures through a second-order meta-time. At one moment of *meta-time* the present is located in 1900, at a later moment in meta-time, the present is located in 1901, at a still later moment, it is located in 1902, and so on. How else *can* we make sense of a present moving along our time-line? Arguably, there is no other way. But have we any reason to believe that another time exists? Of course not. And the problems do not end here. Even if we suppose a meta-time *does* exist, if the defining feature of a temporal (as opposed to spatial) dimension is the presence of a moving present, it seems we need to postulate yet another time-dimension, a meta-meta-time, in order to render intelligible the motion of the meta-present through meta-time. As is clear, we are now launched on an unstoppable infinite regress.

Some suspect difficulties such as these may not prove insuperable, and work on dynamic models of time continues.[6] But undeniably, the most momentous advance in the metaphysics of time to be made in the past century has been the serious and detailed exploration of the *block* view of time, or the *B-theory*. According to the latter, appearances are deceptive, for time does not pass, the present does not move; all moments, all things, all events – past, present and future – are equally real. For the B-theorist, the kinship between time and line runs very deep: time not only has the topological properties of a line, in a key respect it also has the same ontological properties, the same mode of being: just as all points on a line are equally real, so too are the moments of time. And what goes for the moments of time goes for what they contain: the future parts of your life are just as real as the present and past parts.

6
For differing accounts of dynamic time JR Lucas, *The Future*, Oxford: Blackwells, 1989, Storrs McCall, *A Model of the Universe*, Oxford: OUP, 1994, Michael Tooley, *Time, Tense and Causation*, Oxford: OUP, 1977 and Dainton, chapter 1

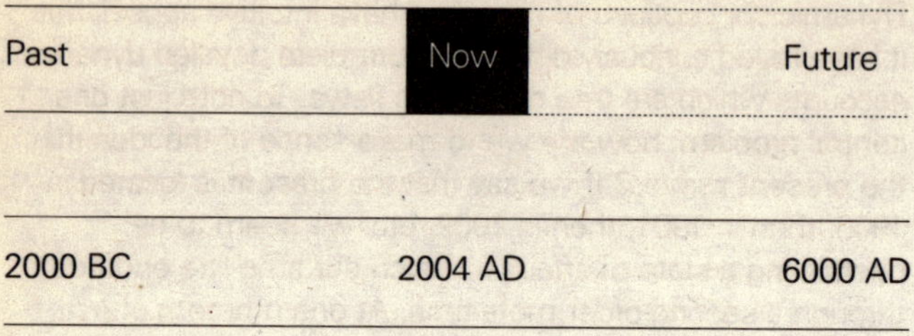

Figure 5
The upper figure depicts a common-sense view of time: the past exists (or is at least fixed), the present is privileged and advancing, the future is as yet unreal. The lower figure depicts the 'block universe' of the B-theory: there is no moving or privileged present, all moments of time are on a par, all are equally real. A B-universe has the ontic character of a line

The B-theory has two powerful advantages over its dynamic competitors. It is consonant with relativistic physics, which relativises simultaneity – and hence the present, to frames of reference – and so makes life difficult for those who regard the present as ontologically privileged, either by being the dividing line between what is real and what is not, or by being the sole locus of being.[7] The B-theory also solves the problem of making sense of a moving present, simply by denying that there is such a thing. Every moment in B-time is a 'present', just as every point in space is a 'here'. But note: accepting the B-theory does not involve the denial of motion or change *per se*, as is sometimes alleged. For the B-theorist, change is perfectly real, it consists in objects having different properties at different times, eg if a person is hungry at noon, but not hungry at 2pm, after having eaten, they have changed. Motion, too, exists. It is simply a matter of objects occupying different spatial locations at different times (or, alternatively, as being differently spatially related to one another at different times).

As is obvious, adopting the B-theory means abandoning some deep-seated beliefs about the nature of time. Rather less obviously, the B-theory sheds new light on the nature of material beings. Our common-sense ontology draws sharp distinction between events or processes which are spread over time, and things which endure through time. Events have *temporal* parts – eg, the first and second halves of a football match – things, as usually conceived, have only *spatial* parts. That your arms and legs are among your parts is obvious; the notion that you-as-you-were-yesterday is one of your parts seems absurd: you existed yesterday, just as you exist today, as a complete human being on both occasions. A thing (as opposed to an extended process) exists as a *whole* at each moment of its career. While this three-dimensionalist way of thinking about persisting things comes naturally to us, it is also rooted in a model of time in which the present is ontologically privileged compared to the past

7

See H Putnam, 'Time and Physical Geometry', *Journal of Philosophy*, 64, 1967, pp 240–7, H Stein, 'On Einstein-Minkowski Space-Time', *Journal of Philosophy*, 65, 1968, pp 5–23 for a now classic exchange on the relationship between the special theory of relativity and ontology and future. If all times are fully real, are we not – in reality – extended four-dimensional beings? From the B-theoretical perspective, we are extended through time in precisely the same way as we are extended through space. According to this new way of thinking – sometimes called perdurantism – we have both spatial and temporal parts. Consequently, when we see a person walking down the street, you are not seeing the whole of that person, you are merely seeing one of their (temporal) parts. The standard ontology – endurantism – regards persisting things as akin to points: they exist as a whole at each moment along the time-line. By contrast, perdurantism regards persisting things as being akin to lines: they are extended through or along the time-line. If, as many B-theorists believe, perdurantism is the true (or better) ontology, the way of thinking which is most faithful to the real nature of things, then we are all more akin to lines than we are accustomed to thinking.[8]

The B-theory is a strikingly clear and simple conception of time, with notable advantages over its competitors, but there are problems still to be solved. Why do we have the impression that we live our lives in a moving present of brief duration if, in reality, our lives are extended like lines across a page? Why, if all moments of time are equally real, do we know more about the past than the future? Progress on these questions has been made. The simple fact that causes precede their effects can explain a good deal. Memories can be viewed as causal effects of earlier experiences, and so the fact that causes precede their effects explains why we can remember the past but not the future, even if our future experiences are just as real as our past experiences. But most B-theorists would concede that mysteries remain, that further work is required.[9] Nonetheless, it may very well be that the kinship between time and line is far more profound than appearances suggest, and many have hitherto thought. If so, our attempt to understand the large-scale structure of the cosmos has been hindered by our failure to appreciate this fact.

[8]
Theodore Sider, *Four-Dimensionalism: An Ontology of Persistence and Time*, Oxford: OUP, 2001, provides an excellent introduction to, and defence of, perdurantism
[9]
Paul Horwich, *Asymmetries in Time*, Cambridge, MA, MIT, 1987, DH Mellor, *Real Time II*, London: Routledge, 1998, Huw Price, *Time's Arrow and Archimedes' Point*, Oxford: OUP, 1996 address these problems in different ways. See also Dainton, chapters 3, 4, 7

Conclusion: Metaphysics and beyond

Our attempts to understand the world are influenced and constrained by our understanding of what is possible, of how a world *could* be or *might* be. In assessing putative possibilities, we rely on the conceivability test: we assume that if a scenario is clearly conceivable, it is possible. Narrowly construed, conceivable means 'contains no inconsistency of a logical or conceptual kind'; construed more broadly it means *imaginable*. Something is imaginable, in the relevant sense, if it can be clearly entertained in our sensory (not necessarily visual) imagination.

As we have seen, so far as our understanding of space is concerned, it may well be that broad conceivability is an unreliable guide to possibility. The ease with which we can imagine pure (immaterial) lines of distance linking objects separated only by void provides the relational conception of space with a legitimacy which may be unwarranted. The fact that the space of our imaginations is three-dimensional and Euclidean renders it hard for us to accept even the possibility of three-dimensional spaces that are non-Euclidean, and mathematics and physics have both suffered as a result. If we could visualise in four dimensions, the possibility of curved three-dimensional space would be perfectly obvious; but since we can't, it isn't.

Time, as usual, raises issues of a different kind, but the general moral is much the same. That a succession of moments has the local topological properties of a succession of points in a line is comparatively uncontroversial, whereas the idea that time could have the ontological properties of a line seems absurd. Here, too, the limits of the imaginable play an important role. Our ordinary experience strongly suggests that only the momentary present is fully real, and that this present is transitory, always on the move, always slipping away. If we try to combine, in our imaginations, this dynamic understanding of temporality with the non-dynamic linear ordering of the B-theory, we simply fail: it cannot be done. But as we have seen, the B-theoretic conception of time may well be the true conception. Time may be more line-like than we are able to imagine.

As is no doubt obvious, these brief considerations have only scratched the surface of the connections between being and line. I have considered some of the ways in which our pre-theoretical grasp of line and linearity influence and impact on our metaphysics, our most general understanding of how things might be. A fuller treatment of even this theme would involve an exploration of Kant's doctrine that space and time are forms of intuition.[10] A more wide-ranging survey of the relevant philosophical work would embrace some of Zeno's notorious and influential paradoxes of motion.[11] But these purely conceptual (or metaphysical) issues do not exhaust the topic, for there are also recent scientific results that are of interest, results that pertain to how things actually are. I can do no more than mention these here, but they *are* certainly worthy of mention.

The four-dimensional conception of enduring things that the B-theory makes possible may render the careers of objects line-*like*. There are developments in current physics which threatens to reduce material beings to lines in a far more literal way. According to string theory, fundamental physical particles are not material points, as long supposed, but vibrating lines, of truly minuscule size. The different modes of vibration – together with the different string-topologies (some are open, some closed) – give rise to the various properties associated with different types of particle. Loop quantum gravity goes still further. Instead of viewing space (or space-time) as a medium which houses material particles, this theory construes space itself as a web of intersecting lines – a conception which combines elements of the traditional substantival and relational theories in a novel way.[12]

10

Immanuel Kant, *Prolegomena to Any Future Metaphysics*, (ed.) Gary Hatfield, Cambridge: CUP, 1997 and Michael Friedman, *Kant and the Exact Sciences*, Harvard: Harvard University Press, 1992

11

Wesley C Salmon, *Zeno's Paradoxes*, Indiana: Hackett Publishing, 2001

12

Brian Greene, *The Elegant Universe*, London: Jonathan Cape, 1999 and Lee Smolin *Three Roads to Quantum Gravity*, London: Weidenfeld and Nicolson, 2000

Both these theories are at the highly speculative frontier of theoretical physics, and future developments may take a quite different turn. But as things stand, the notion that our entire universe may be entirely constructed of nothing but line-like elements certainly has to be taken seriously. If so, the relationship between line and reality would be intimate indeed, and rather more far-reaching than previously suspected.

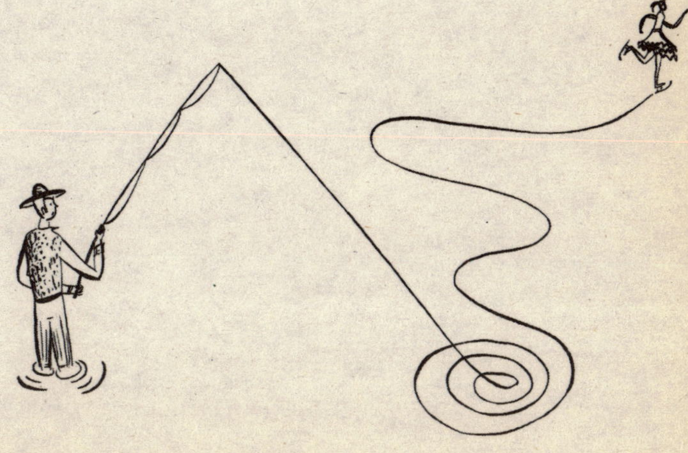

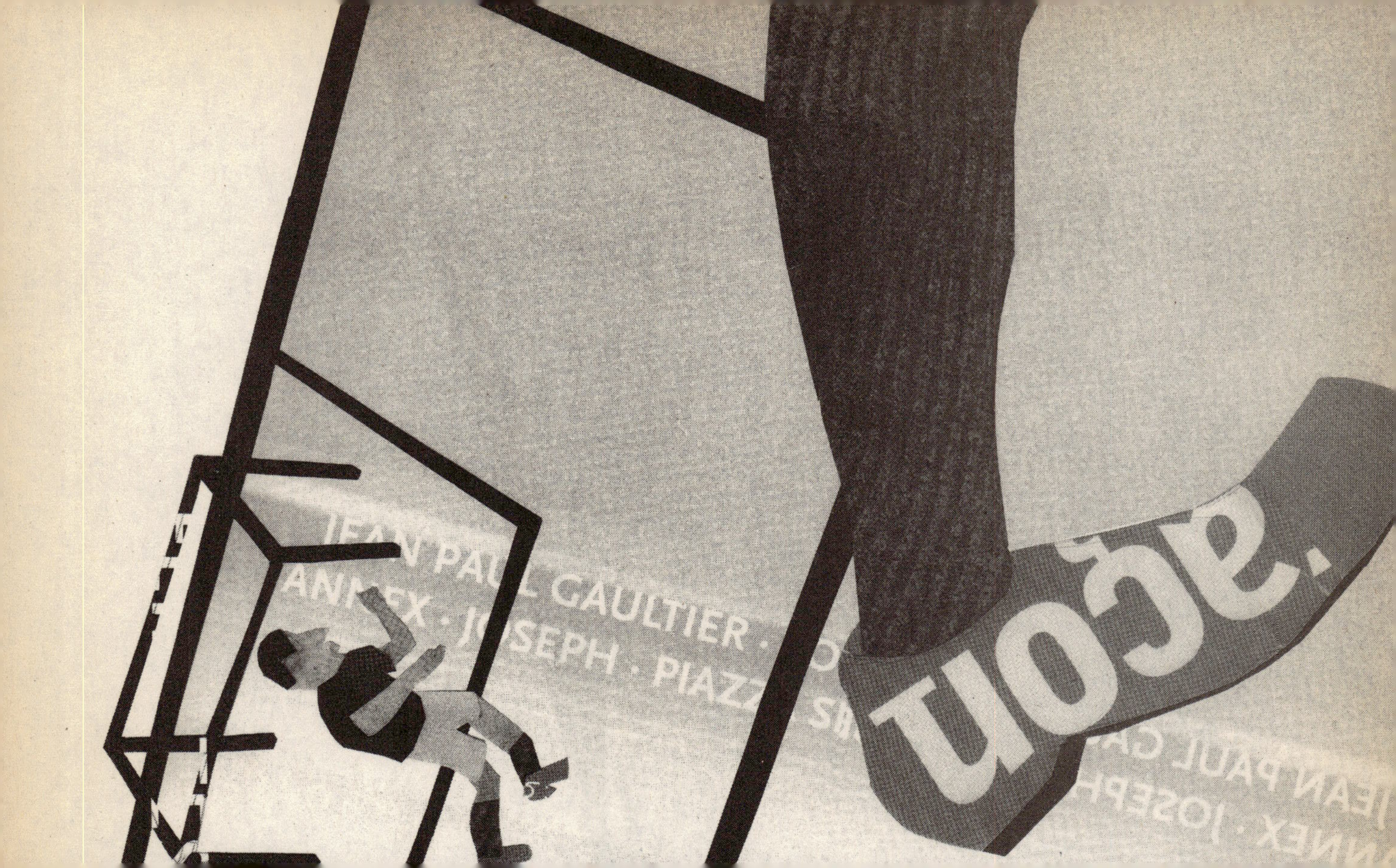
JEAN PAUL GAULTIER · ANNEX · JOSEPH · PIAZZA
JEAN PAUL GAULTIER · ANNEX · JOSEPH

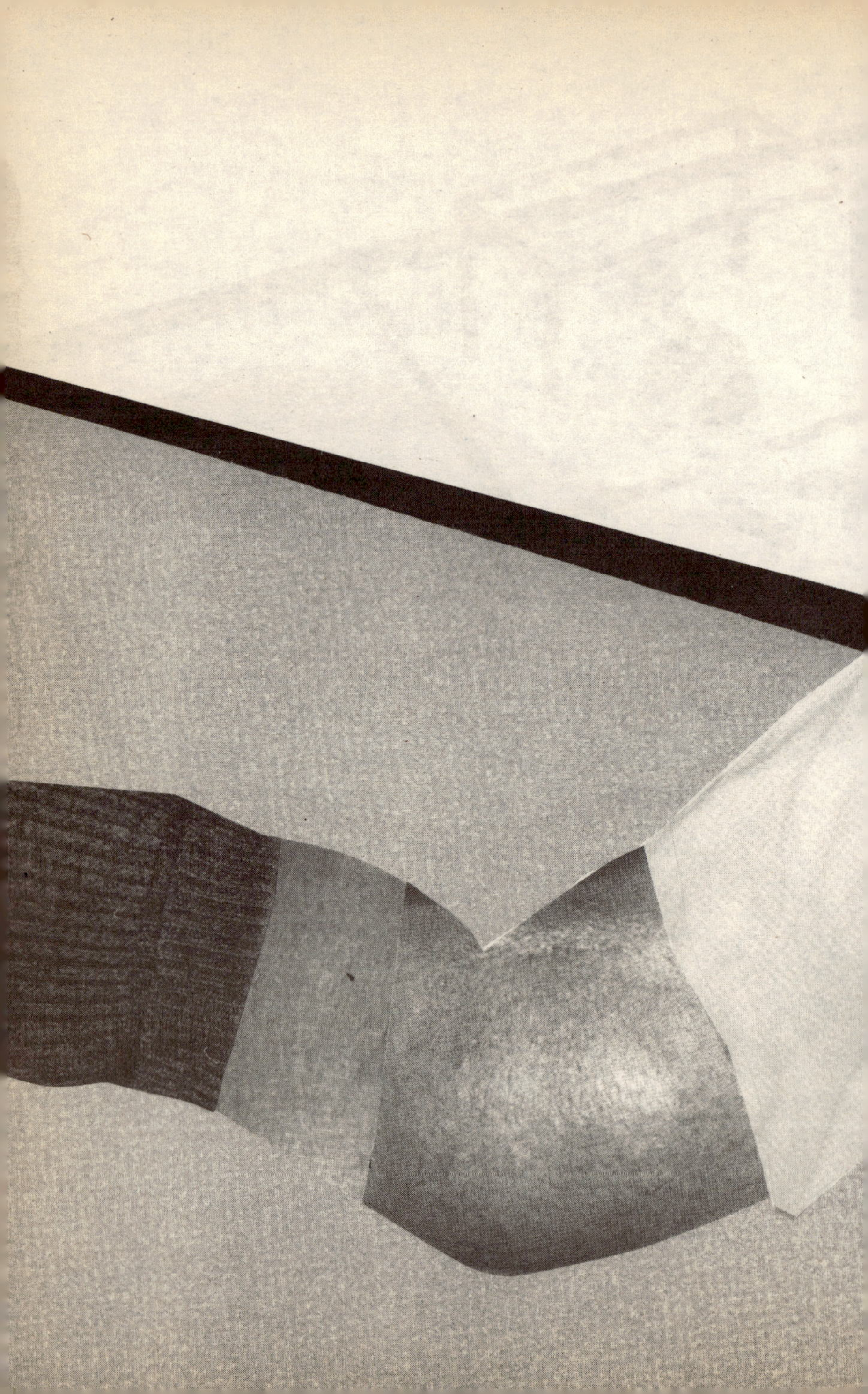

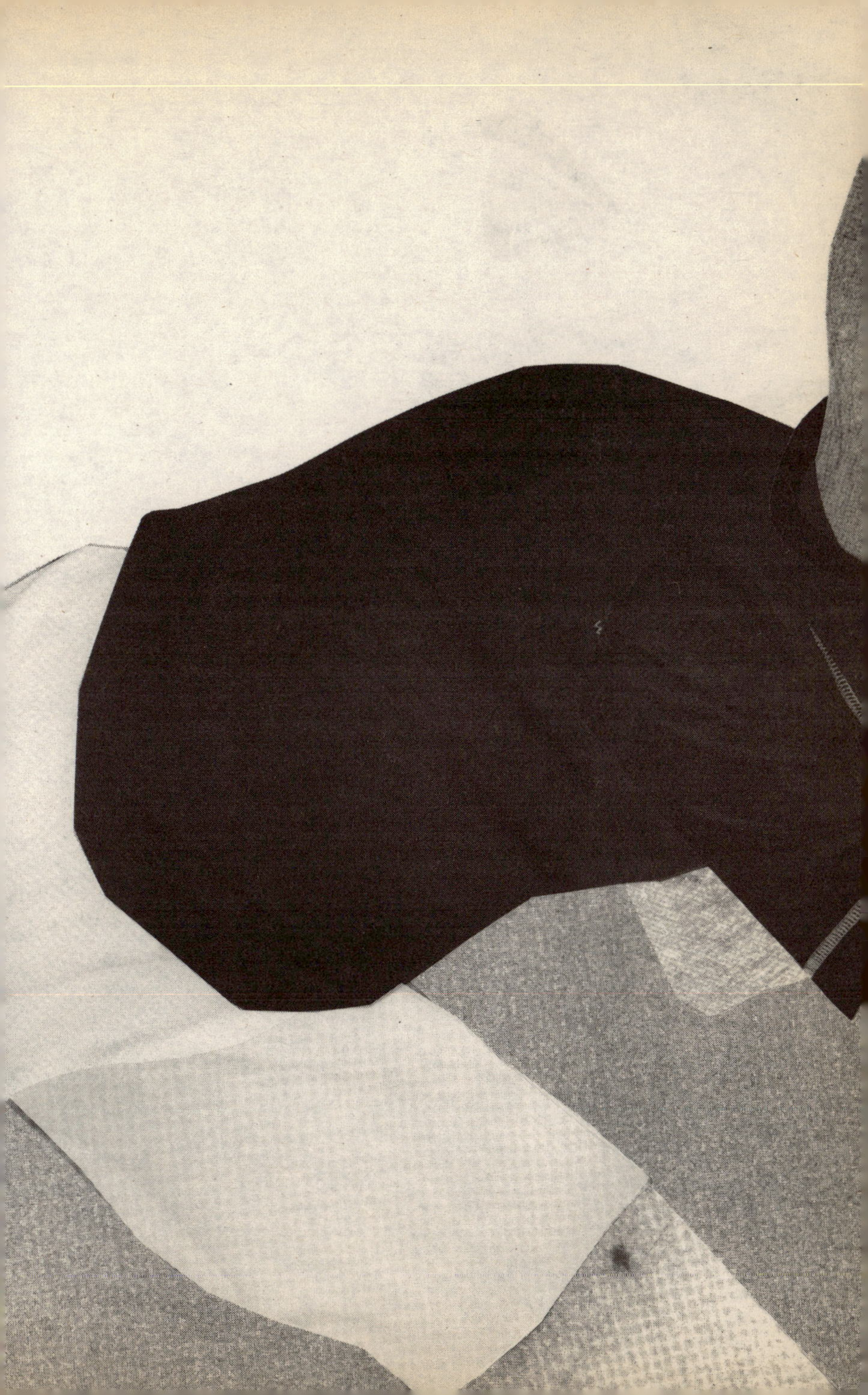

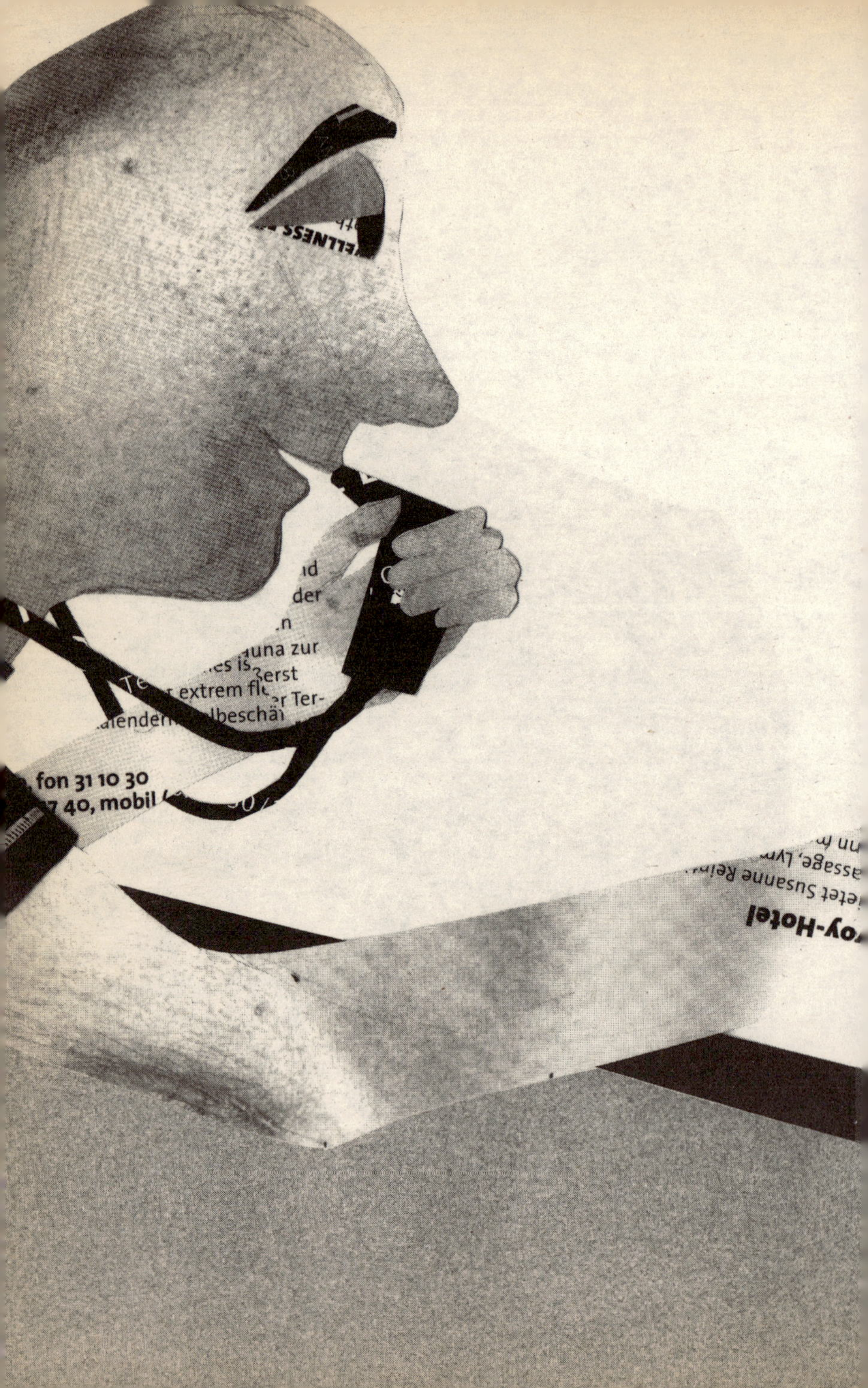
 WELLNESS
der
n
una zur
es is
er extrem fl...er Ter-
...enden...lbeschä...
fon 31 10 30
7 40, mobil
...tet Susanne Rei...
...assage, Ly...
...voy-Hotel

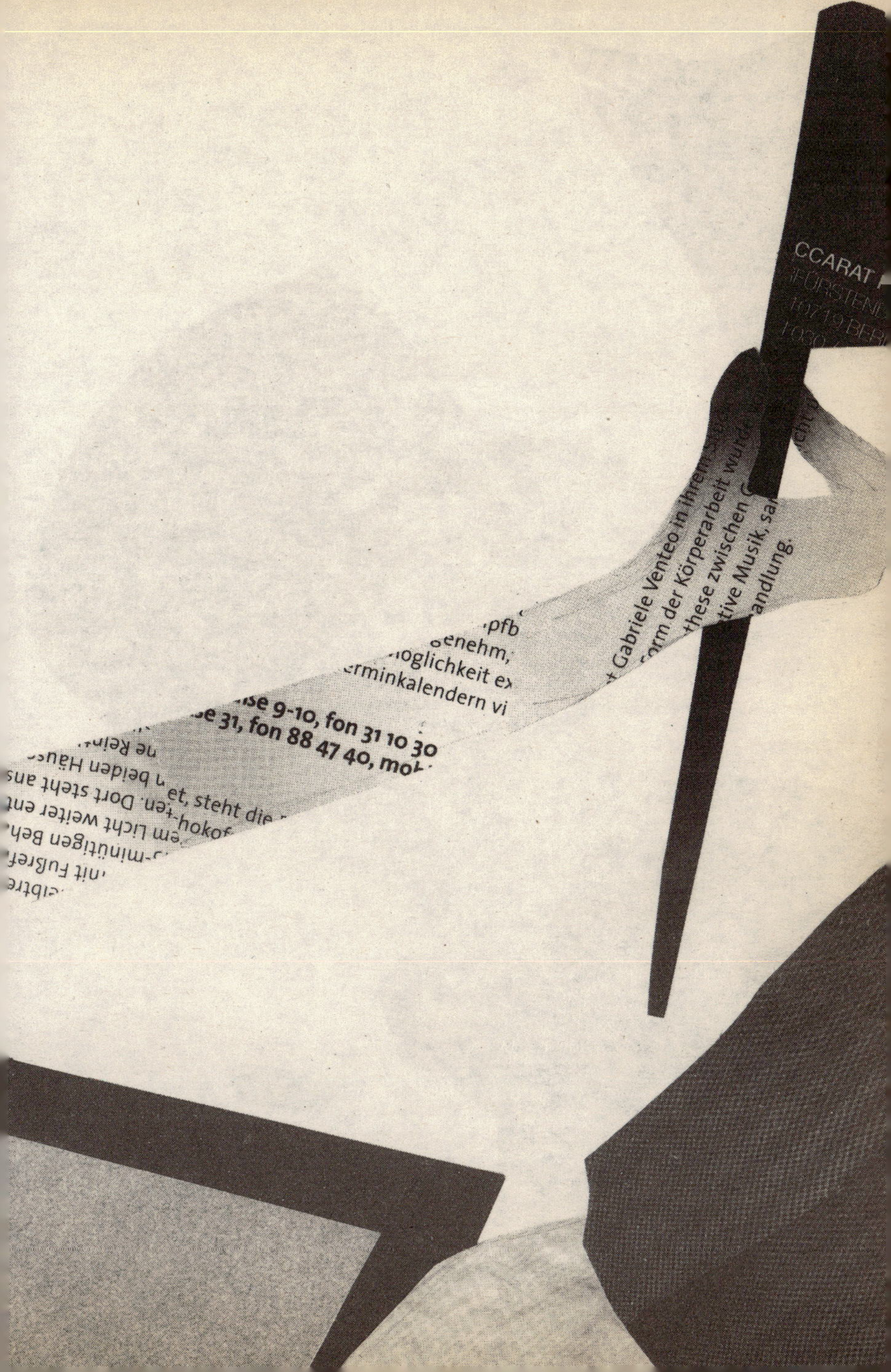

CCARAT
FÜRSTEN[...]
10719 BER[...]
1930

[...]t Gabriele Venteo in ihrem [...]
[...]rm der Körperarbeit wurde [...]
[...]these zwischen [...]
[...]tive Musik, sa[...]
[...]andlung.

[...]pfb
[...]enehm,
[...]öglichkeit ex
[...]erminkalendern vi
[...]se 9-10, fon 31 10 30
[...]se 31, fon 88 47 40, mo[...]
[...]et, steht die [...]
[...]ne Rein[...]
[...]n beiden Häus[...]
[...]hoku-[...]en, Dort steht ans[...]
[...]em Licht weiter ent[...]
[...]-minütigen Beh[...]
[...]nit Fußref[...]
[...]ibtre[...]

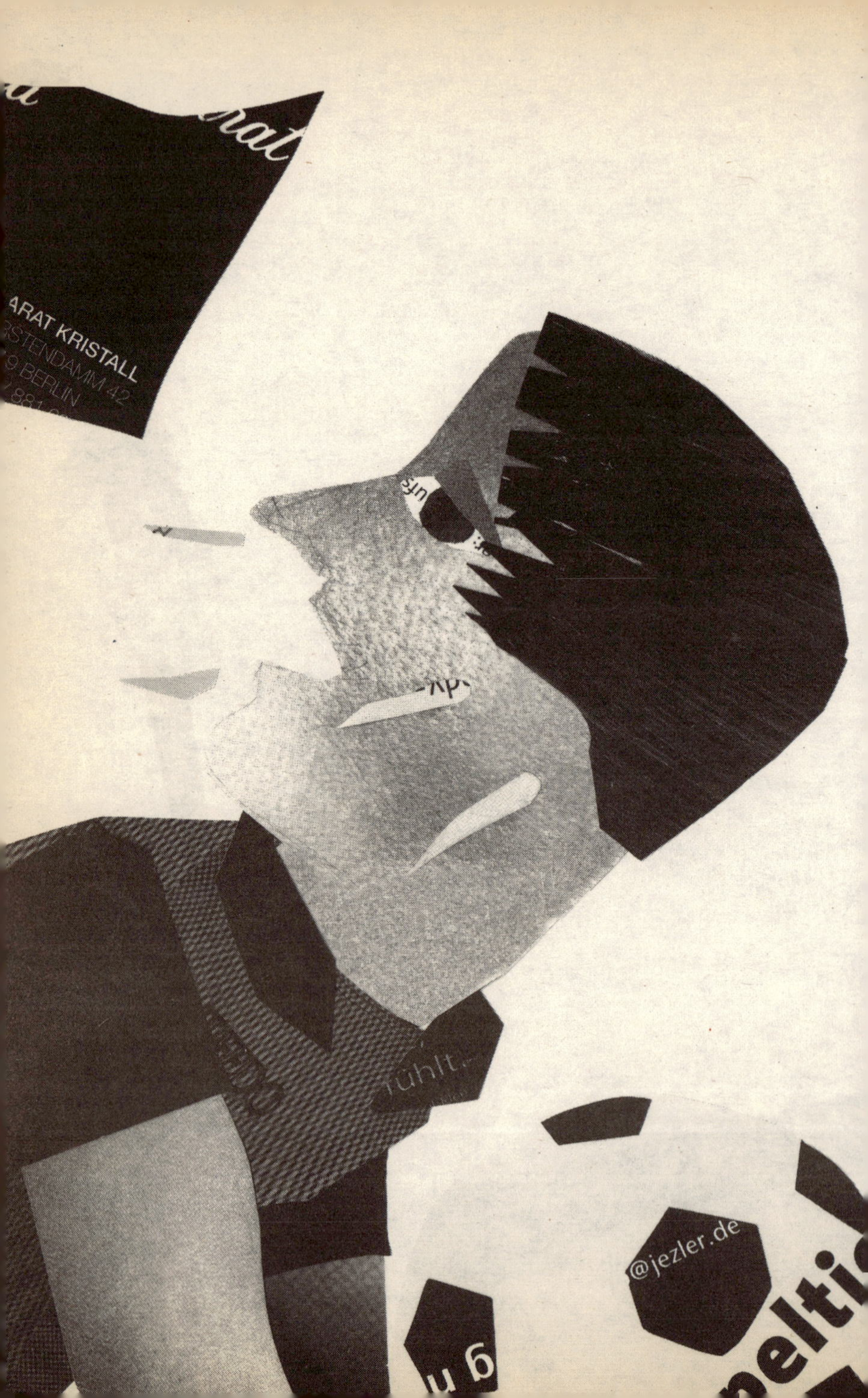
ARAT KRISTALL
STENDAMM 42
9 BERLIN
881
@jezler.de

Each of Alfred Hitchcock's three key masterpieces – *Vertigo*, *North-by-Northwest*, *Psycho* – can be conceived as the full visual and narrative deployment of the most elementary fact of drawing a line, a different line in each case. This specific line is prefigured already in the credits sequence: in *Vertigo*, it is the vertiginous circular line turning into itself; in *North-by-Northwest*, it is the multitude of intersecting parallel horizontal and vertical lines; in *Psycho*, it is, of course, a fragmented line, a line cut into bits. One can thus claim that this visual motif stands for what Jacques Lacan called a *sinthom*, the minimal formal pattern which encapsulates the libidinal investment that sustains the consistency of a work.

There is, however, another line which precedes this elementary formal matrix and opens up the space for it – the line which cuts the very depicted narrative reality, designating the inscription of the gaze into it. About one-third of the way into Hitchcock's *Shadow of a Doubt*, there is a brief passage which fully bears witness to his genius: the young FBI detective investigating Uncle Charlie takes his young niece Charlie out for a date; we see them in a couple of shots walking along the streets, laughing and talking vivaciously - then, unexpectedly, we get a fast fade-out into the American shot of Charlie in a state of shock, gaping with a transfixed gaze at the detective off screen, blurting out nervously, 'I know what you are really! You are a detective!'… Of course, we do expect the detective to use the opportunity to acquaint Charlie with Uncle Charlie's dark side. However, what we expect is a gradual passage: the detective should first break the cheerful mood and address the serious issue, thus provoking Charlie's outburst when she realises how she was being manipulated (the detective asked her for a date not because he liked her, but as part of his professional work). Instead of this expected gradual passage, we are directly confronted with the traumatised Charlie. (One could argue that, with her shocked gaze, Charlie does not react to some previous detective's words: what happened is that, in the middle of the frivolous conversation, she all of a sudden grasps that there is something other than flirting going on. However, even in this case, the standard procedure to film the scene would have been to show the couple pleasantly talking; then, all of a sudden, Charlie would be struck by the fateful insight. The key Hitchcockian effect would thus be missing: the direct jump to the shocked gaze.) It is only *after* this shocking discontinuity that the detective voices his suspicions about Uncle Charlie's murderous past.

To put it in temporal terms: it is as if, in this scene, the effect precedes its cause, that is, we are first shown the effect (the traumatised gaze) and then given the context responsible for this traumatic impact – or are we? Is the relationship between cause and effect really inverted here? What if the gaze is here not merely a recipient of the event? What if it somehow mysteriously generates the perceived incident? What if the conversation that follows is ultimately an attempt to symbolise/domesticate this traumatic incident? Such a cut in the continuous texture of reality, such a momentous inversion of the proper temporal order, signals the intervention of the Real. If the scene were to be shot in the linear order (first the cause, then the effect), the texture of reality would have been left undamaged. That is to say, the Real is discernible in the gap between the true cause of the terrified gaze and what we are given to see later as its cause: the true cause of the terrified gaze is not what we are shown or told afterwards, but the fantasised, traumatic excess 'projected' by the gaze into the perceived reality.

A more complex example of the same procedure is one of the key recurring Hitchcockian motifs, that of a couple arguing on a small hill, half-barren, with a few trees and bushes, usually windy, just outside the scope of the public place populated by a group of ignorant observers. For Alain Bergala, this scene stages Adam and Eve in the Garden of Eden, just prior to being chased from it, in the process of tasting the forbidden knowledge.[1] If one discounts a couple of minor references and variations (from *Notorious* to *Topaz*), there are three main versions of it: *Suspicion*, *The Birds*, and *Torn Curtain*. In *Suspicion*, it is the brief shot of Grant and Fontaine struggling on a windy hill near the church, observed by Fontaine's friend from the entrance to the church. In *The Birds*, it is the scene, just prior to the first bird attack on the group of children, in which Mitch and Melanie withdraw to

1

Alain Bergala, 'Alfred, Adam and Eve', in, *Hitchcock and Art: Fatal Coincidences* (accompanying volume to the Centre Pompidou exposition), (eds.) Dominique Paini and Guy Cogeval, Paris and Milano: Centre Pompidou and Mazotta, 2001, pp 111 – 25

a small hill above the picnic place where children are celebrating a birthday party. Finally, in *Torn Curtain*, it is the scene in which Newman and Andrews withdraw to a small hill, out of earshot of the East German secret police officials who can only observe them – there, Newman explains to his fiancée the truth about his mission.

The key feature is that, in all three cases, the couple on the hill is observed by an innocent/threatening/ignorant observer below the hill (friends close to the church; Mitch's ex-lover and mother; East German secret policemen) who sees only the scene and is unable to discern the meaning of the intense exchange of the observed couple. The traumatic character of the scene, the excess of the Real that pertains to it, hinges on this gaze: it is only from the standpoint of this gaze that the scene is traumatic. When, later, the camera jumps closer to the couple, the situation is again 'normalised'. Bergala is right to emphasise how this scene reproduces the basic coordinates of the child's primordial sexual encounter: witnessing the parents' love making, unable to decide what the scene he sees is (violence or love?). The problem of his account is simply that it appears all too close to the standard 'archetypal' reading, trying to identify the kernel of the meaning of the scene instead of conceiving of it as a meaningless *sinthome*. The fundamental lesson of this procedure is that there is more truth in this misperception by the partial gaze than in the 'objective', true state of things. This gap is rendered palpable by the fantasmatic opening scene of *Beau Geste* (William Wellman), the classic Hollywood adventure melodrama from 1939: the mysterious desert fortress in which there is no living person, only dead soldiers placed on its walls, a true desert counterpart to the spectre of the ship floating around without any crew. Towards its end, *Beau Geste* renders the same sequence from within the fortress, namely, it depicts how this haunting image of the fortress with dead soldiers was generated. The key point here is the *excess* of this scene of illusory appearance: its libidinal force overpowers its later rational explanation. And, does the same not also go for Hitchcock's *Vertigo*?

Like *Beau Geste*, the focus of *Vertigo* is on creating the perfect semblance, which is then explained away. Furthermore, the whole point is that, when we learn the 'true story', the first part of the movie (until Madeleine's suicide) is *not* simply explained away as a fake – there is more truth in the appearance than in the true story behind it. Truth has the structure of a fiction, which is why we often pay the price for getting involved in a fake appearance in flesh, by death. Playing with appearances *is* playing with fire. This is why the crucial question of *Vertigo* is: 'But how real is Elster?' Like the Judge in Kieslowski's *Red*, is Elster not, as to his libidinal status, the fantasy product of the hero's imagination? This fits well into the reading of *Vertigo* as a film that plays upon two registers:

'On the one hand, it is a carefully crafted 'yarn,' the story of the character, Scottie, of what happens to him, and of how he responds, located in a detailed and recognisable California environment. On the other hand, it is famously dreamlike both in its texture and in the way it introduces story and protagonist. Echoing Robin Wood, James Maxfield argues that 'everything after the opening sequence is… dream or fantasy'.[2]

In the second reading, the structure is the one of Ambrose Bierce's famous short story 'An Occurrence at Owl Creek Bridge,' in which everything that follows the hanging of a man at the story's outset is, at the end, revealed as the fantasy of the dying man. This structure is also recognisable in films like *Point Blank*, which is often read as depicting the fantasy of the mortally wounded Lee Marvin. The crucial point here is to identify what Deleuze would have called the 'dark precursors', the non-repeated, unique elements which, precisely insofar as they belong only to one level, serve as the bridge, mediator, or point of passage between the two. The point is not so much to identify the stand-in for reality within fantasy (like, in *Vanilla Sky*, the doctor from real life who appears within the hero's digitally generated universe to warn him), but, rather, the stand-in for the 'illusory' mental universe within 'reality' itself.

2
Charles Barr, *Vertigo*, London: BFI Classics, 2002, p 77

The gap and, simultaneously, link between the two levels is rendered palpable in the mysterious moments of the perfect timing of the interrupting intrusion of the third agency. In the pivotal and, perhaps, most beautiful scene of the film, that of Scottie and Madeleine in his apartment, after he saves her from drowning under the Golden Gate Bridge: 'As their talk grows more intimate, Scottie offers to get her more coffee, and reaches for her cup; their hands touch, and we can see, within a two-shot, that for both of them this is a moment of erotic tension and possibility. Immediately, the phone rings, the tension is broken, and Scottie leaves the room to answer it. When he returns, she has gone. The call is, of course, from Elster, and its timing is uncannily precise, to the second, allowing them to get so far but no further.'[3]

One should accomplish here a crucial step further into the disintegration of fantasy – the moment when the line we are talking about gets blurred, so that a separate uncanny spectral domain appears which is neither reality nor fantasy. David Lynch's *Mulholland Drive* perfectly depicts this gradual disintegration. The two main stages of this process are, first, the excessively intense acting in the test scene, and, then, when the autonomous partial object ('organ without a body') emerges in the scene in the nightclub Silencio. The movement is here from the excess which is still contained in reality, although already disturbing it, sticking out of it, to its full autonomisation, which causes the disintegration of reality itself: say, from the pathological distortion of a mouth to the mouth leaving the body and floating around as a spectral partial object (the same as in Syberberg's *Parsifal*, where we pass from the wound on the body to the wound as autonomous organ without a body, outside it). This excess is what Lacan calls *lamella*, the infinitely plastic object that can transpose itself from one to another medium: from excessive (trans-semantic) scream to a stain (or anamorphic visual distortion). Is this not what takes place in Munch's *Scream*? The scream is silent, a bone stuck in the throat, a stoppage which cannot be vocalised and can only express itself in the guise of a silent visual distortion, curving the space around the screaming subject.

[3]
Barr, *op.cit.*, p 59

In Silencio, where Betty and Rita go after successfully making love, a singer sings Roy Orbison's 'Crying' in Spanish. When the singer collapses, the song goes on. At this point, the fantasy collapses too – *not* in the sense that 'the mist dissipates and we are back in sober reality,' but, rather, in the sense that–from within, as it were – fantasy loses its mooring in reality and gets autonomised, as a pure spectral apparition of a bodiless 'undead' voice (a rendering of the Real of the Voice similar to that at the beginning of Sergio Leone's *Once Upon a Time in America*, in which we see a phone ringing loudly, and, when a hands picks up the receiver, the ringing goes on). The shot of the voice continuing to sing even when its bodily support collapses is the inversion of the famous Balanchine ballet staging of a short piece by Webern: in this staging, the dancing goes on even after the music stops. We have thus, in one case, the voice that insists even when deprived of its bodily support, and, in the other case, the bodily movements that insist even when deprived of their vocal (musical) support. The effect is not simply symmetrical, because, in the first case, we have the undead vocal drive, the immortal life, going on, while, in the second case, the figures which continue to dance are 'dead men dancing,' shadows deprived of their life-substance. However, in both cases, what we witness is the dissociation between reality and the real; in both cases, the Real insists even when reality disintegrates. This real, of course, is the fantasmatic Real at its purest. And, to put it in Deleuzian terms, is this 'autonomisation' of the partial object not the very moment of the extraction of the virtual from the actual? The status of the 'organ without the body' is that of the virtual – in other words, in the opposition between the virtual and the actual, the Lacanian Real is on the side of the virtual.

Of course, in all of these cases, the shock-effect is followed by an explanation that relocates it back within ordinary reality. In the nightclub scene in *Mulholland Drive*, we are warned at the very outset that we are listening to pre-recorded music, that the singers just mimic the act of singing; in the case from Leone, the phone we continue to hear ringing after the receiver is picked up is another phone, etc.

However, what is nonetheless crucial is that, for a short moment, part of reality was (mis)perceived as a nightmarish apparition – and, in a way, this apparition was 'more real than reality itself' since, in it, the Real shone through. In short, one should discern which part of reality is 'transfunctionalised' through fantasy, so that, although it is part of reality, it is perceived in a fictional mode. Much more difficult than to denounce/unmask (what appears as) reality as fiction is to recognise in 'real' reality the part of fiction. Is this not what happens in transference, in which, while we relate to a 'real person' in front of us, we effectively relate to the fiction of, say, our father? Recall also *Home Alone*, especially part two: in both parts, there is a cut two-thirds into the film; although the story seems to take place in a continuous diegetic place, it is clear that, with the final confrontation between the small kid and the two robbers, we enter a different ontological realm, a plastic cartoon-space in which there is no death, in which my head can explode, yet I go on as normal in the next scene… Again, part of reality is here fictionalised.

It is such a fictionalised partial object that also serves as the support of voice. In his advice to young composers, Richard Wagner wrote that, after elaborating the contours of the musical piece one wants to compose, one should erase everything and just focus one's mind on a lone head floating freely in a dark void, and wait for the moment when this white apparition starts to move its lips and sing – this music should be the germ of the work to be composed. Is this procedure not that of getting the partial object to sing? It is not a person (a subject) – the object itself should start to sing.

At the beginning of Monteverdi's *Orfeo*, the goddess of music introduces herself with the words 'Io sono la musica…'- is this not something which soon afterwards, when 'psychological' subjects had invaded the stage, became unthinkable, or, rather, unrepresentable? One had to wait until the 1930s for such strange creatures to reappear on the stage. In Bertolt Brecht's 'learning plays,' an actor enters the stage and addresses the public: 'I am a capitalist. I'll now approach a worker and try to deceive him with my talk of the equity of capitalism…' The charm of this procedure resides in the psychologically 'impossible' combination, in one and the same actor, of two distinct roles, as if a person from the play's diegetic reality can also, from time to time, step outside himself and utter 'objective' comments about his acts and attitudes. This second role is the descendant of Prologue, a unique figure which often appears in Shakespeare, but which later disappears with the advent of psychological-realist theatre: an actor who, at the beginning, between the scenes or at the end, addresses the public directly with explanatory comments, didactic or ironic points about the play, etc. Prologue thus effectively functions as the Freudian '*Vorstellungs-Repraesentanz* /representative of representing': an element which, on stage, within its diegetic reality of representation, holds the place of the mechanism of representing as such, thereby introducing the moment of distance, interpretation, ironic comment – and, for that reason, it had to disappear with the victory of psychological realism. Things are here even more complex than in a naive version of Brecht: the uncanny effect of Prologue does not hinge on the fact that he 'disturbs the stage illusion' but, on the contrary, on the fact that he does *not* disturb it. Notwithstanding his comments and their effect of 'extraneation' we, the spectators, are still able to participate in the stage illusion. And, this is how one should also locate Lacan's '*c'est moi, la vérité, qui parle*' from his '*La Chose freudienne*':[4] as the same shocking emergence of a word where one would not expect it. Therein resides the traumatic impact of this shift: the distance between the Other and the Thing is momentarily suspended, and it is the Thing itself which starts to speak. One cannot help but recall here Marx's version of Lacan's '*c'est moi, la vérité, qui parle*', his famous 'Let us imagine that a commodity would start to speak…' from *Capital*: here also, the key to the logic of commodity fetishism is provided by the fictive 'magic' of an object starting to talk.

This notion of the partial object that starts to talk is also the site of forceful ideological investments, especially with regard to the way the male gaze endeavours to counter the fundamental hystericity (lie, lack of a firm position of enunciation) of the feminine speech.

<hr>

4
See Jacques Lacan, *Ecrits*, Paris: Editions du Seuil, 1966, p 409

In his extraordinary philosophical novel *Les Bijoux indiscrets* (1748), Denis Diderot renders the ultimate fantasmatic answer:[5] a woman speaks with *two* voices. The first one, that of her soul (mind and heart), is constitutively lying, deceiving, covering up her promiscuity; it is only the second voice, that of her *bijou* (the pearl which, of course, is her vagina itself), which, by definition, *always* speaks the truth – a boring, repetitive, automatic, 'mechanical' truth, but truth nonetheless, the truth about her unconstrained voluptuousness. This notion of the 'talking vagina' is not meant as a metaphor, but quite literally: Diderot provides the anatomical description of vagina as instrument *a corde et a vent* capable of emitting sounds. (He even reports on a medical experiment: after excising the entire vagina from the body, doctors tried to 'make it talk' blowing through it and using it as a string.) This, then, would be one of the meanings of Lacan's *la femme n'existe pas*: there are no talking vaginas directly telling the truth; there is only the elusive, lying, hysterical subject.

Does, however, this mean that the concept of the talking vagina is a useless one, just a sexual-ideological fantasy? A closer reading of Diderot is necessary here: his thesis is not simply that the woman has two souls, one – superficial, deceiving – expressing itself through her mouth, and the other through her vagina. What speaks through a woman's mouth is her Soul that desperately tries to dominate her bodily organs. And, as Diderot makes clear, what speaks through her vagina is not the Body as such, but precisely the vagina as *organ*, as a subjectless partial object. The speaking vagina thus has to be inserted into the same series as the autonomised hand in *Fight Club* and *Me, Myself and Irene*. It is in this sense that, in the case of the talking vagina, it is not the woman, the feminine subject, who compulsively tells the truth about herself. It is, rather, the truth itself that speaks when her vagina starts to talk: 'It's me, the truth, which speaks here' – me, and not I. What speaks through the vagina is drive, this asubjective *moi*.

5

Denis Diderot, 'Les Bijoux indiscrets', in, *Oeuvres completes*, Vol 3, Paris: Hermann, 1978. I rely here on Miran Bozovic, 'Diderot and l'ame-machine', in, *Filozofski vestnik 3*, Ljubljana, 2001

The ultimate *perverse* vision would have been that the entire human body, inclusive of the head, is nothing but a combination of such partial organs – the head itself is reduced to just another partial organ of *jouissance*, as in those unique utopian moments of hard-core pornography, when the very unity of the bodily self-experience is magically dissolved, so that the spectator perceives the bodies of the actors not as unified totalities, but as a kind of vaguely co-ordinated agglomerate of partial objects: here the mouth, there a breast, over there the anus, close to it the vaginal opening… The effect of close-up shots and of the strangely twisted and contorted bodies of the actors is to deprive these bodies of their unity – somewhat like the body of a circus clown, which the clown himself perceives as a composite of partial organs that he fails to co-ordinate completely, so that some parts of his body seem to lead their own particular lives (suffice it to recall the standard stage number in which the clown raises his hand, but the upper part of the hand doesn't obey his will and continues to dangle loosely). This change of the body into a desubjectivised multitude of partial objects is accomplished when, for example, a woman is in bed with two men and does fellatio on one of them, not in the standard way, actively sucking his penis, but so that she lies flat on a bed and leans her head over its edge downwards into the air. When the man is penetrating her, her mouth is above her eyes, the face is turned upside-down, and the effect is one of an uncanny transformation of the human face, the seat of subjectivity, into a kind of impersonal sucking machine being pumped by the man's penis. The other man is, meanwhile, working on her vagina, which is also elevated above her head and thus asserted as an autonomous center of *jouissance* not subordinated to the head. The woman's body is thus transformed into a multitude of 'organs without a body', machines of *jouissance*, while the men working on it are also desubjectivised, instrumentalised, reduced to workers serving these different partial objects. Within such a scene, even when a vagina talks, it is just a 'talking head' in the same way that any other organ just exerts its function of *jouissance*. This perverse vision of body as a multitude of the sites of partial drives, however, is condemned to failure: it disavows castration.

There is, of course, a vast contemporary literary and art tradition concerning the talking vagina – from the French cult film of 1975 *Le sexe qui parle* 'Pussy Talk' (Frederic Lansac and Francis Leroi) to Eve Elsner's recent notorious monodrama *The Vagina Monologues*. However, what happens here is precisely the wrong step: the vagina is subjectivised, transformed into the site of woman's true subjectivity – in Elsner, sometimes ironic, sometimes desperate… it is *The* Woman who speaks through her vagina, not vagina-truth itself which speaks. It is for this precise reason that *The Vagina Monologues* remains caught in the logic of bourgeois subjectivity. If we are to look for a place where the subversive potential of an object starting to speak is unleashed, we have to look elsewhere.

In the middle of David Fincher's *Fight Club* (1999), there is an almost unbearably painful scene, worthy of the weirdest David Lynch moments, which serves as a kind of clue for the film's final surprising twist. In order to blackmail his boss into continuing to pay him even after he quits working, the hero throws himself around the man's office, beating himself bloody before the building's security officers arrive. In front of his embarrassed boss, the narrator thus enacts upon himself the boss's aggression towards him. The only similar case of self-beating is found in *Me, Myself and Irene*, in which Jim Carrey beats himself up – here, of course, in a comic (although painfully exaggerated) way, as one part of a split personality pounding the other part. In both films, the self-beating begins with the hero's hand acquiring a life of its own, escaping the hero's control – in short, turning into a partial object, or, to put it in Deleuze's terms, into *an organ without a body* (the obverse of the body without an organ). This provides the key to the figure of the double with whom, in both films, the hero is fighting: the double, the hero's Ideal-Ego, a spectral/invisible hallucinatory entity, is not simply external to the hero – its efficacy is inscribed within the hero's body itself as the autonomization of one of its organs (hand). The hand acting on its own is the drive ignoring the dialectic of the subject's desire: drive is fundamentally the insistence of an undead 'organ without a body', standing, like Lacan's lamella, for that which the subject had to lose in order to subjectivise itself in the symbolic space of the sexual difference.

What, then, does the self-beating in *Fight Club* stand for? If, following Fanon, we define political violence not as opposed to work, but, precisely, as the ultimate political version of the 'work of the negative', of the Hegelian process of *Bildung*, of the educational self-formation, then violence should primarily be conceived as self-violence, as a violent re-formation of the very substance of the subject's being. Therein resides the lesson of *Fight Club*:

'First, one has the difficulty of emancipating oneself from one's chains; and, ultimately, one has to emancipate oneself from this emancipation too! Each of us has to suffer, though in greatly different ways, from the chain sickness, even after he has broken the chains.'[6]

In many of the smaller American cities with a large unemployed working class population, something which uncannily resembles *Fight Club* has recently emerged: 'toughman-fights', in which only amateur men (and also women) engage in violent boxing matches, getting their faces bloody, testing their limits. The point is not to win (losers are often more popular than winners), but, rather, to persist, to continue standing on one's feet, not to remain lying on the floor. Although these fights stand under the sign of 'God bless America!' and are perceived by (most of) the participants themselves as part of the 'war on terror', one should not immediately dismiss them as symptomatic of a redneck 'proto-Fascist' tendency: they are part of a potentially redemptive disciplinary drive. So when, in *Fight Club*, after a bloody fight, the hero comments 'This was a near-life experience!' (thereby reversing the standard phrase 'a near-death experience'), is this not an indication that fighting brings the participants close to the excess-of-life over and above the simple run of life – in the Paulinian sense, they are *alive*?

6
Friedrich Nietzsche, in a letter to a friend (dated July 1882), quoted in, Bryan Magge, *The Tristan Chord*, New York: Henry Holt and Company, 2000, p 333

What, then, does it mean, exactly, that the (partial) object itself starts to speak? It is not that this object is subjectless, but that this object is the correlate of the 'pure' subject prior to subjectivisation. Subjectivisation refers to the 'whole person' as the correlate of the body, while the 'pure' subject refers to the partial object alone. When the object starts to speak, what we hear is the voice of the monstrous, impersonal, empty-machinic subject that does not yet involve subjectivisation (the assumption of an experienced universe of sense). One should bear in mind here that the two couples, subject-object and person-thing, form a Greimasian semiotic square. That is to say, if we take 'subject' as the starting point, there are two opposites to it: its contrary (counterpart) is, of course, 'object', but, its 'contradiction' is a 'person' (the 'pathological' wealth of inner life as opposed to the void of pure subjectivity). In a symmetrical way, the opposite counterpart to a 'person' is a 'thing', and its 'contradiction' is the subject. 'Thing' is something embedded in a concrete life-world, in which the entire wealth of the meaning of the life-world echoes, while 'object' is an 'abstraction', something extracted from its embeddedness in the life-world.

One should bear in mind here how the Freudian notion of the 'partial object' is not that of an element or constituent of the body, but of an organ which *resists* its inclusion within the Whole of a body. This object, which is the correlate of the subject, is the subject's stand-in within the order of objectivity: it is the proverbial 'piece of flesh', the part of the subject that the subject had to renounce in order to subjectivise itself, to emerge as subject. Was this not what Marx was aiming at when he wrote about the rise of the class-consciousness of the proletariat? Does this also not mean that the commodity 'working force' which, on the market, is reduced to an object to be exchanged, starts to speak?

Here is the shortest Jacob and Wilhelm Grimm fairy tale, *The Willful Child*:

'Once upon a time there was a child who was willful and did not do what his mother wanted. For this reason God was displeased with him and caused him to become ill, and no doctor could help him, and in a short time he lay on his deathbed. He was lowered into a grave and covered with earth, but his little arm suddenly came forth and reached up, and it didn't help when they put it back in and put fresh earth over it, for the little arm always came out again. So the mother herself had to go to the grave and beat the little arm with a switch, and as soon as she had done that, it withdrew, and the child finally came to rest beneath the earth.'

Is this obstinacy that persists even beyond death not freedom – death drive – at its most elementary? Instead of condemning it, should we not rather celebrate it as the ultimate resort of our resistance? This, then, is the ultimate line to be drawn, the line which makes subjectivity emerge: the line between the body and its organ, the cutting line of the 'symbolic castration' which liberates an organ from the constraints of the body.

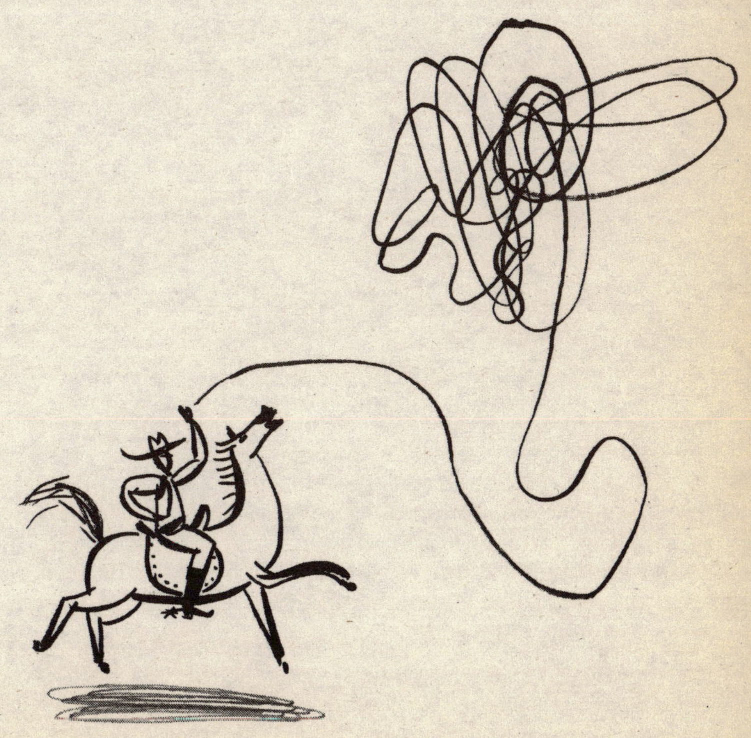

Text and line in figurated poems and calligrams　81
Christophe Marchand-Kiss

A simple definition: the word calligram derives from the Greek *kallos* for beauty and *gramma* for 'letter' or 'writing'. The calligram is a '*poème dont les vers sont disposés de façon à former un dessin évoquant le même objet que le texte*'.[1] The calligram introduces both a tension and a *symbiosis* between a text and a drawing. One cannot untangle the text within the body of the calligram from the drawing, bounding the text. The text *goes* over the drawing, and the drawing *goes* over the text. The drawing is a tracing of the text, and the text a tracing of the drawing. Both of these tracings overlap each other creating one thing (it is a question of transparency) that is neither a text nor a drawing, but a calligram.

When the text elsewhere runs, it folds there. When the drawing elsewhere follows a line it follows words. When the text is a representation of itself and is represented, the drawing shows the text 'itself'. So there are two kinds of constraints, either the text submits itself to the shape of the drawing or the drawing organises the text. But one cannot help thinking that the balance or the cancellation of any dichotomy between the text and the drawing (at least any *opposition* between forms), if one can imagine it, one cannot conceive it. First, one looks at a calligram or a figurated poem, then one reads it. The text is *subordinate* to the drawing. The shape of the drawing as an image, initially attracts the eye, pushing the text back inside the perimeter of the drawing to form the drawing's outermost edges, and yet, if there is only a drawing without a text, there is no calligram at all. One is the slave of the other. One cannot exist without the other. Therefore the calligram is closely linked to a series of subtle subordinations, which cancel out neither the drawing or the text, as a process of successive overlappings. The calligram does not say 'things twice (when once would doubtless do)',[2] as Michel Foucault claims, it says plenty of things which multiply according to various angles and one of these angles hides all the others.

[1] Petit Robert, *Dictionnaires le Robert*, 1993, p 324. 'The calligram is a poem of which the arrangement of the verses forms a drawing which evokes the same object as the text' (author's translation)

[2] Michel Foucault, *This is not a Pipe*, translated and edited by James Harkness, Berkeley, University of California Press, 1983, p 24

For instance, within *The Egg*, from Simias of Rhodes,[3] a poet
from the **Alexandrian** period, under Ptolemy II, the drawing,
like the **text are one and** the same gift which the 'egg-shape'
has **to undertake to pass** it on. The content (the text) is
inscribed in the container (the drawing), the container arises
from the content. In other words, the content *is* the
container (the text forms the drawing) as the container *is*
the content (the drawing forms the text, the verse has to
make the egg). This is all evident and true, but the text is
not the 'egg', it exhausts again and again the egg-shape, but
without success, exceeding the egg in itself, but constantly
remaining below it. It is inside and outside the egg.

It seems that many relationships are formed
between the 'egg as a text' and the 'egg as a drawing'. Yet
they never succeed (or they do incompletely) in being tied
together as they are not able to be untied. To tie the 'egg as a
text' and the 'egg as a drawing' (the text and its drawing are
not dissociated) means that there is no movement backwards
(a dissociation of the text and its drawing) or forwards
(a perfect appropriateness between both).

One might say that the text is *corrupted* by the
shape, because it determines it. The container is more in
evidence than the content. To know the ancient Greek
changes nothing, it is a text with an egg shape that we look
at. A container with a content, if not illusory, at least ancillary
and annexed. This visible simultaneity of the text and the
drawing, not in its creation but in its result, the fact that the
text can suggest the drawing and the drawing mark the text
out, explain, in part the reason why there is not an exact
superimposition of both. The calligram creates a space of
loss, a gap, a void secreted within the making of the figurated
poem, which is only revealed through the process of reading.
This loss, this gap and this void never alter but remain
constant, like a sort of no man's land, where the text and the
drawing stand *below*, there without *being* there, never at the
same time except in the material illusion of the page.

[3] Simias of Rhodes, 'The Egg', in, *Theocritus, Vetustissimorum authorum georgica, bucolica et gnomica poemata quae supersunt*, (ed.) Joanne Crispino, Geneva, Bibliothèque nationale de France, 1569. We knows nothing of Simias apart from three poems: The Axe, The Wings and The Egg written in rhopalic verses that Meleager collected in an anthology in the 1st century BC, then republished in a different form by Constantin Cephalas in the ninth century

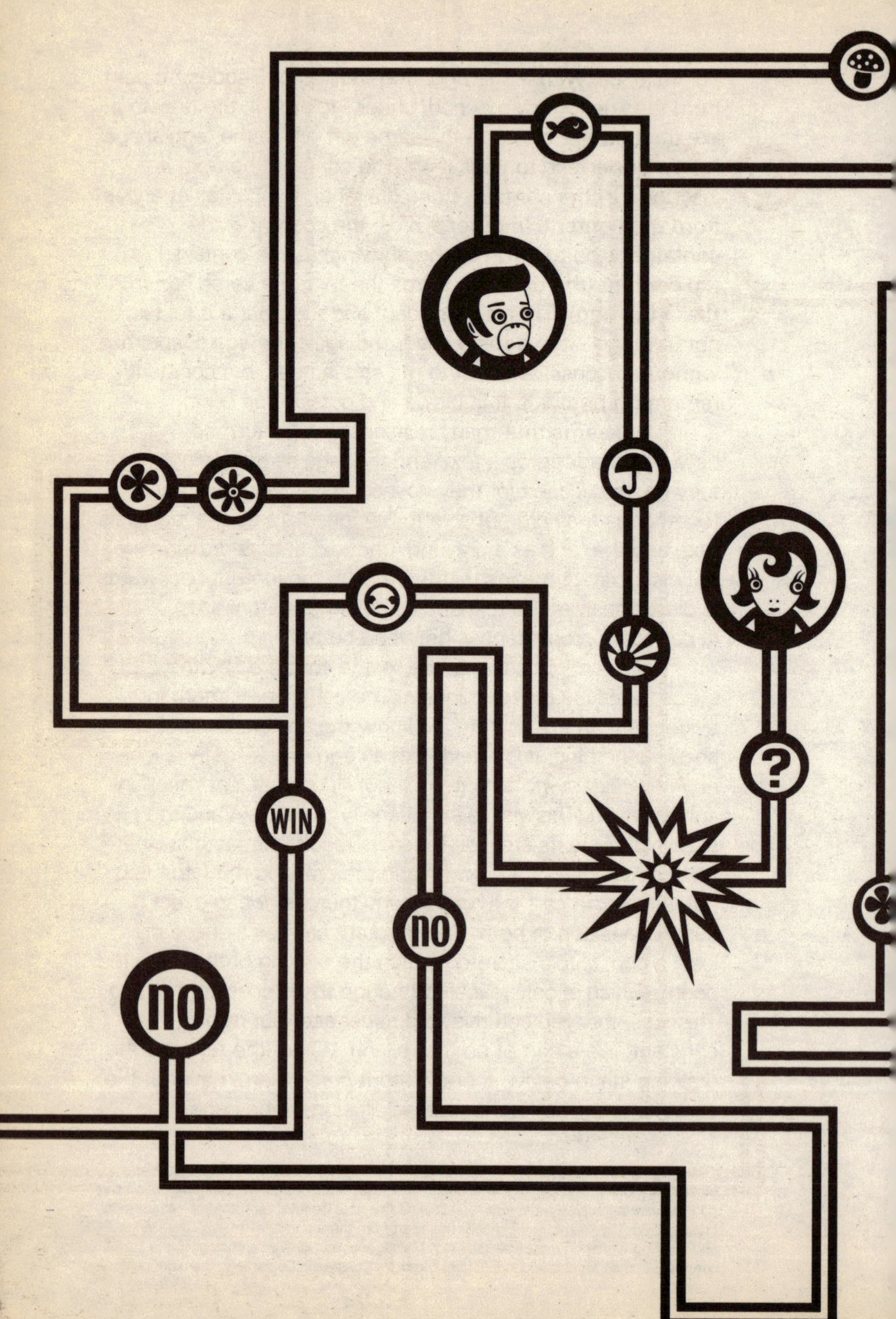

WIN
no
no

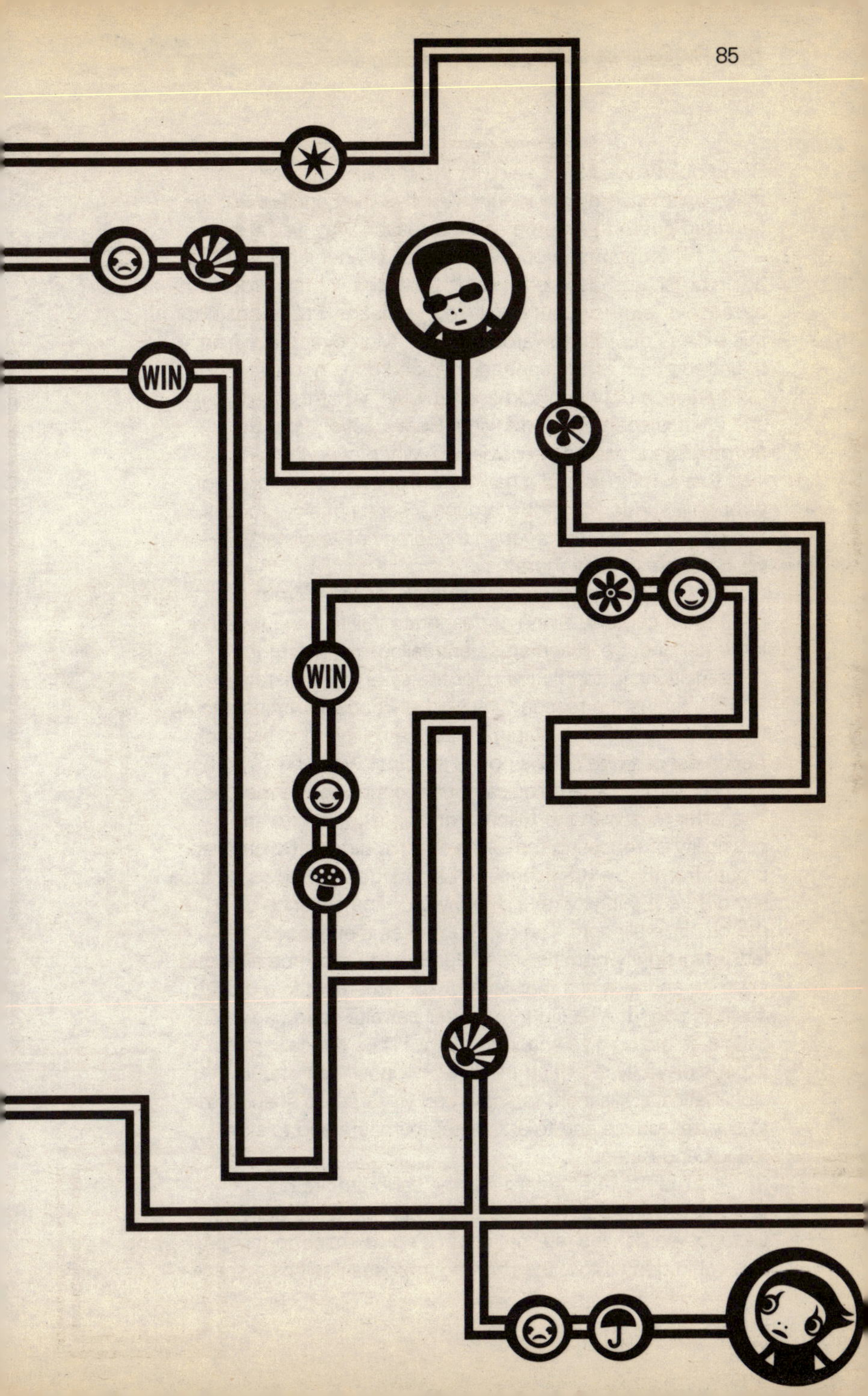

Being *below*, we might say that the text and the drawing
make up an incomplete whole, which is the condition for the
figurated poem to emerge and the reason why it puzzles.

The figurated poem is disorder, even if it is meant to
be an order. It is disorder through an *excess* of this order, not
because it refutes it, but because the means it uses tips out
this excess of order towards disorder. Moreover the *whole*
figurated poem is this contradiction and does not fulfil it.
Contradiction between text and drawing, what the text says
and what is seen of the drawing. Contradiction from its
distorted and twisted interweaving, when everything must
lead to a symbiosis and a harmony. But everything fails, not
through a sudden gap, but through a series of slow moves.
In a certain sense, the *sudden* modernity of Apollinaire's
calligram are already there.

Only in a certain sense though, because from the
nineteenth century, a kind of desperate will to bring together
the letter and the image arose and failed, increasing the
contradictions (often flagrant) for the sake of consistency.

That is the reason why Michel Foucault writing about
the paintings of René Magritte and the calligram in his book
Ceci n'est pas une pipe is not as succinct when he says that
the calligram is… 'tautological. But in opposition to rhetoric.
The latter toys with the fullness of language. It uses the
possibility of repeating the same thing in different words, and
profits from the extra richness of language that allows us to
say different things with a single word. The essence of
rhetoric is in allegory. The calligram uses that capacity of
letters to signify both as linear elements that can be arranged
in space and as signs that must unroll according to a unique
chain of sound. As a sign, the letter permits us to fix words;
as line, it lets us give shape to things. Thus the calligram
aspires playfully to efface the oldest oppositions of our
alphabetical civilisation: to show and to name; to shape and
to say; reproduce and to articulate; to imitate and to signify;
to look and to read.'[4]

The figurated poem like the calligram are not
tautologies, and if it might be likely that 'the letter permits
us to fix words' and 'as line, it lets us give shape to things',
one could deny it too: the drawing imposes itself as a shape

or a line and fixes the words. And it is precisely because
it takes advantage of 'the extra richness' that it cannot
'(to) show and (to) say; (to) reproduce and (to) articulate',
because its movement is never simultaneous.

On the contrary it distributes an 'extra load', this
excess the author of a figurated poem or a calligram is not
able to control because the drawing of a lute (for example)
is never a lute, and this lute drawn by 'the line of the letters'
is even well short of its own representation. It is a
representation of the lute *minus* the text which follows its
outlines. As an effect of a sharing out, both of the elements
of the figurated poem or the calligram, linked by a sort of
excessive 'extra load' and abundance of contradictory signs
that finally take away from each other through the difference
of representation, yet without a separation.

The marriage between the drawing and the text is
not impossible, but unlikely. For each the chain of signs is
different, their structures, rhythms, speeds and intensities,
cannot lead to an addition. 1 plus 1 or 'one is equal to two',
a sort of double text which *doubles* the drawing and a
drawing which doubles the text but to a subtraction, 1 minus
$1 = 0$, sum of the *points* of convergence between a drawing
and a text, a shape and a poem. It is a paradox that one
obtains with figurated poems and calligrams a sort of
divergent unity, the unique sum, equal to zero of a
hypothetical merging. If the line is at the same time a *verse*
of the poem and an outline of the drawing, it does not say the
same thing twice. It reveals first a little of the drawing; then a
little of the poem; and even if it says it in the same space, it is
never in the same time. The figurated poem and the calligram
do not part from each other in space, but in time, and it is
there that the subtraction *appears* without being represented.

However, in their inseparability, the first, either
the text or drawing, must dare to darken the other, if not
ultimately to erase it. The figurated poem becomes in turn
just a drawing again (an altar, a palm), so the viewer can *fully*
enjoy its aesthetic qualities, or just a poem, so the reader can
be convinced, not only aesthetically (here it is only incidental)
but also politically (the poem is tricky, it has to use rhetoric)
of the poems intentions.

The figurated poem is no more than a poem in itself (through
a full deconstruction of its contradictory signs), as it *remains*
also a poem into the page (a material illusion). Then there are
two movements: the vision of an object (a drawing plus an
unread text equals a figurated poem drawn by letters, no
matter what words are seen, no matter their order, their
meaning as there is no discourse) and the reading of a text
are this object and at the same time make it disappear.
Michel Foucault understood that very well when he wrote:
'For the text to shape itself, for all it juxtaposed signs to form
a dove, a flower, or a rainstorm, the gaze must refrain from
any possible reading. Letters must remain points, sentence
lines, paragraphs surfaces or masses–wings, stalks, or petals.
The text must say nothing to this gazing subject who is a
viewer, not a reader. As soon as he begins to read, in fact,
shape dissipates. All around the recognised word and the
comprehended sentence, the other graphisms take flight,
carrying with them the visible plenitude of shape and leaving
only the linear, successive unfurling of meaning–not one drop
of rain falling after another, much less a feather or a torn-off
leaf. Despite appearances, in forming a bird, a flower, or rain,
the calligram does not say: These things *are* a dove, a flower,
a downpour. As soon as it begins to do so, to speak and
convey meaning, the bird has already flown, the rain has
evaporated.'[5]

    Maybe this is the 'tragedy' of the figurated poem and
the calligram, both being there and not *totally* being there.
The figurated poem and the calligram disappear as one
cannot look at the calligram and read the words contained
within the calligram, at the same moment (or in the same
movement). Therefore there is a question of temporalities
which evolve in a different mental space. This space, through
the practice of looking, turns 'it rains' into rain (child's
universe) and then through reading, turns the rain (same
child's universe) into 'it rains' (and one reads it only obliquely),
The letters are *at once* a drawing with lines and points, which
turn into a discourse when this drawing becomes a more or
less geometrical shape. These letters are each time identical,
but they are not inscribed into the same temporality and fill
two different spaces: a mental and a physical one.

That is why Paul Zumthor is right to claim that '*le dessin remplit la fonction d'un titre; d'un cadre où s'inscrit le discours*', but is wrong to notice, even if it is about some particular calligram (the Carolingian *carmen figuratum*) that '*le dessin surgit de l'intérieur, il est texte lui-même (...)*'.[6] The drawing, instead of 'surgir de lintérieur', emerges for the viewer from outside through the immediate recognition of an indistinct (or distinct) shape which on this account *takes shape* before him or her: but the text is not fully visible for him or her yet. The figurated poem and the calligram, when they are seen, remove the text and when they are read, erase the drawing.

Guillaume Apollinaire's calligram, published for the first time in the *Soirées de Paris*, in 1914 under the name of 'idéogrammes lyriques', have a great expressiveness by the tension he created between the drawing and the text, by allowing the reader to simultaneously keep one eye on the drawing and one eye on the text. The same is true for the tree and the cigar-smoking of *Paysage* in *Calligrammes*, and for the *Crux* (which was red, maybe) where it is written that '*elle (Lou) soigne les blessés de la guerre*' in *Poèmes à Lou*.[7] However, if we are able to keep one eye on the drawing and one eye on the text, it is both because of the iconic familiarity of the image and because the path of the reader's eyes realises the drawing, simply by following the text along the body of the drawing.

5

Michel Foucault, *op. cit.*, p 24

6

Paul Zumthor, 'Carmina figurata: une mode carolingienne', in, *Change*, no. 4, Paris, Seuil, 1969. 'The drawing acts as a title; a frame where comes a discourse.' (...) 'The drawing comes out from outside; it is a text itself' (translated by the author)

7

Guillaume Apollinaire, 'Poèmes à Lou', in, *Œuvres poétiques*, La Pléiade, éditions Gallimard, 1965, p 379

We know that the text does not coincide with the drawing. 'It rains' is not the rain, but a modal value of 'to rain', and the rain is not [an oblique line] but a reminiscence like a stylisation of the rain. In another connection, the words '*un CIGare allumé qui fum*' in *Paysage*, draws the cigar and its burning tip with '*un CIGare a*' and the smoke with '*Ilumé qui fum*'. '*Ilumé*'[8] would be in a mimetic way, a sort of extension of the burning tip of the cigar and not the beginning of a wreath of smoke.

When the drawing in the figurated poem shows enough so the name of the object comes straightaway to our mind, even if we do not read the poem, that it is not the same for some of Apollinaire's calligrams, which sometimes reveal some uncertainty as to what the drawing signifies, which is only ever fully revealed through the reading of the poem. One of the three objects in *La mandoline, lœillet et le bambou* reminds us of a flower (because the carnation 'l'œillet' cannot be the two other objects) but which one?[9]

Is the man with spread arms and legs in *Paysage* lying down? Does he run? Does he gesture with his hand? (A gesture of victory?) A lot of ambiguities remain. In fact, the words and their arrangement through the space of the page are of great importance for Apollinaire, as they bring *incidentally*, a drawing *recognisable as an object*. The best of his calligrams are like this: from *Lettre-Océan* to *Voyage* and *La petite auto,*[10] because they exceed the 'calligram category' and meet a tradition from Sterne to Mallarmé and renew it through the typographic and collage experiments of the beginning of the twentieth century.

After Apollinaire (and generally from the end of the Second World War), the calligram is a part of visual poetry now. The word is mainly considered in its materiality. In Eugen Gomriger's poetry,[11] a calligram is not a text or a drawing but only a word indicating a 'direction' and a meaning like in *Wind*, (or Ernst Jandl's work the word 'Film', unwinds like a roll of… film. The words truncated and the letters

8
Guillaume Apollinaire, *Calligrammes, op.cit.*, p 170
9
Guillaume Apollinaire, *Calligrammes, op.cit.*, p 209
10
Guillaume Apollinaire, *Calligrammes, op.cit.*, respectively pp 183–98 and 207
11
Eugen Gomriger, *Kosntellationen*, Ideogramme, Studenbuch, Reclam, 1977, p 82

reversed *film* becomes *flim* for, maybe, Flimmerkiste in German, telly in English, or *flimmerkisten*, to twinkle.) In Reinhardt Döhl's calligrams,[13] the word *Apfel* (apple) takes the shape of an apple, like the word *Wurm* (a worm) takes the shape of a worm in the apple, a worm one has to look for a long time… and in many others, like Jean-François Bory's *Un carré de soie tissé artisanalement dans le quartier dUtano à Kyoto*[14] or Ian Hamilton Finlay,[15] who, in *Village* turns the v upside down and transforms it into a house with a sloping roof. This materiality of the word is still more obvious in Anna Banana's visual poetry: a text is going to be written on the body of a man (a stick photography) and turns gradually into a body itself as this one turns into a text (*Cavellini writes his history at the waterfall*),[16] or in e.e. cummings' poetry, with the poem *XLV* from *W(ViVa)*: its arrangement evokes a small piece of window pane through which a lonely man watches the passers-by along the street; a small and dirty piece of window pane which is darkened by the words making it up.[17]

It is finally the margin between language and the object, what one says and what one sees and their representation that is in question. A gap that the figurated poem like the calligram cannot fill in. Like in *Le plongeoir de Narcisse of Michel Leiris*[18] where the name of the writer draws the frame of a mirror, at the centre of which there is nothing at all.

12
Ernst Jandl, *Sprechblasen*, Reclam, 1979, p 86

13
Reinhard Döhl, 'Apfel', in, *Konkrete Poesie*, Deutschsprachige Autoren, Anthologie von Eugen Gomriger, Reclam, 1972, p 38

14
Jean-François Bory, *Retour au Japon, calligrammes et fragments de journalintime*, Edition à durée limitée, 1996

15
Ian Hamilton Finlay, 'Village', in, *Text Buchstabe Bild*, Zürcher Kunstgesellschaft, Helmhaus Zürich, 1970, p 43

16
Anne Banana, 'Cavellini writes his history at the waterfall', in, *Poesia Totale*, 1897–1997, dal colpo di dadi alla poesia visuale, Pallazzo delle ragione, Mantova, (eds.) Enrico Mascelloni and Adriano Sarenco, Parise Publisher, 1997, p 627

17
e.e. cummings, *Complete Poems (1904–1962)*, (ed.) George Firmage, Liveright, 1991, p 355

18
Michel Leiris, *Mots sans mémoire*, Gallimard, 1969, p 115. Michel Leiris was fascinated by the word calligram, but he never accepted that one designates by this word his 'combinations of words with the shape of a drawing'

Gridlock

1

All footnotes are set in 8.45 point interline space so that lines 1, 5, 9, 13, etc correspond with the top of a grid unit

Gridlock

Spatula is based on a page grid consisting of 12 x 4 units.
The type is set in Univers 45, the size is 9 point
interline with 11.25 point space, so that all lines correspond
with the top of a grid unit.

Figure 1
All captions are set
in 8.45 point interline
space so that lines
1, 5, 9, 13, etc
correspond with the
top of a grid unit

Spatula is based on a page grid consisting of 12 x 4 units.

For three days now, I have sat in front of this same sheet
of paper, just staring at it.

      The surface of the paper appears to be so
unbelievably white, clean, untouched, perfect and yes, so
pure. Yet I am certain that this is an illusion. For I am also
dimly aware that the paper's all too apparent hygiene masks
a dirty secret, a permanent cloying stain, that simply will not
go away.[1]

      Today though, I cannot tell you why, but something
has changed and so, I draw a line.[2]

I draw sitting at a table.

While drawing I am surrounded by many objects, the largest of which is the building I inhabit, in which I now sit in a small compartment of the overall object. Within my compartment there are many smaller objects, that appear to have a utilitarian function and so remain largely silent, others, though, need only a glance in their general direction, to invite a litany of unresolved stories to remorselessly pour out. To be able to draw though, I have to, over the space of two or three days, construct a veil to cover the constant clamour that surrounds me. I have to silence all.

It is only within this silence that I am really able to draw.

I have found that if I stare at the paper's surface constantly
for a matter of hours, something starts to happen to the
material relation I have to the paper as a discrete object and
to the physically unbreachable horizon line across its surface.
During these moments of intensity, I experience a dissolution
of a certain sense of self, as I am slowly dissolved, into the
glaring light of the simultaneous space contained within the
picture. As a quotidian element situated within the walls of
my compartment, a piece of paper on first reading may
appear physically and mnemonically dead. I certainly find that
all objects are dead to my gaze. Although, if I stop my casual
wandering and sit silently alone and I let my eyes drift long
enough along the body of an object, I sometimes find that
the surface begins to dematerialise, first into a gooey writhing
miasma and then slowly, slowly clearing, into an empty,
frozen and still space, located somewhere within the object.
I have found though during these moments of plastic
fascination, that there is something wholly distinct about
paper as 'ground'. Which perhaps through the relentless
appropriation by a pictorial tradition, which having read the
painterly surface as an imaginary fissure, a tear in the
continuum, allows a path into an imaginative arena, far
surpassing the potentialities of all other objects.

Out of nowhere.

Flowing out between pen and paper, line describes
the path of my arm as if in a diagram. To bring a line into the
world of the material, all I have to do is bring one object into
contact with another and record the trajectory of a
movement. This inaugural moment as a line is physically
(re)born, establishes a character to line, as forever resident
between things generally.

1

'The success of what we call "sublimation" relies on this reflexive reversal of the "lack of
the signifier" into the "signifier of lack" – that is to say, on this primordial metaphor by
means of which the stain – the brute enjoyment of which there is no signifier – is replaced
by an empty signifier, a signifier which does not signify any reality – that is to say: a stand-in
for a representation which is constitutively excluded from reality, which must fall out if
"reality" is to retain its consistency' Slavoj Žižek, 'In His Bold gaze My Ruin Is Writ Large',
in, *Everything You Always Wanted To Know About Lacan (But Were Afraid To Ask Hitchcock)*,
(ed.) Slavoj Žižek, London and New York: Verso, 1992, p 239

2

The accompanying drawings which form part of this article, are details of a series of graphite
studies by the author

This liminal character, which sees line as always held between categories, can first be observed within the duration of the bodily gesture required to draw, as line is momentarily held between pen and paper. Secondly, a singular line is situated equidistant to the eight contra fields as described in figure 1, that are created by the simple act of inscribing a line upon a two-dimensional surface, which held apart only by an ideal spacing, allow distinctions to emerge from what was once before, this inaugural act of inscription, an inchoate flow of impressions. This simple grammar, the banal ordinances of line inferred upon, within and before the event horizon of the picture plane, enable an ensemble of three-dimensional relations to begin to speak, prior to signification. After which, all relations between lines are only ever either to the left, right, below or above a singular line or oblique of that line or behind, in front, upon or within the body of the line. In this sense, line commands a spatial array of relations solely in respect to itself, by placing the eye of the beholder not at the centre, but spaced-out on the periphery, as line inhabiting the sovereign middle ground is both marginal to the construction of meaning; line is always seen to reside between distinctions and yet is also central, in that this very same line also offers us the promise of inscribing meaning upon the lack we experience on encountering the papers void potentiality.

Finally, an ensemble of lines, held in mutual relation, allow a complex set of actions to be planned and realised, both within the modalities of the industrial and aesthetic economies. Relational lines allow a series of visual codes to be projected upon the observable regularity of the space between lines, thereby creating the ability for lines to communicate across language divisions, by signifying the universal and, hence, simple condition of existence, shared by all distinctions, as that of being one object spaced between other objects. Broadly speaking, relational line ensembles fall into two categories, descriptive geometry and aleatoric drawing.[3]

[3] For a detailed reading of the language of line within architectural representation permit me to refer the reader to: Gordon Shrigley, *Insignificance, A Short Discourse on the Physical and Ideational Economy of Line within Architectural Representation*, Stuttgart: Solitude Editions, 1998

Both 'instrumental' and 'aesthetic' practices of line though, hold their respective positions in respect to each other, only by denying to the extent to which they are both caught up within the same visual ideology. In that the distinction which still holds today between the 'applied' and 'non-applied' drawing, is only maintained to the extent that one is seen to adhere to a hygienic theory of representation, as line is employed as if it were a dumb neutral historically transcendent tool, without inherent characteristics. Leaving more consciously aleatoric practices to distinguish themselves only by overtly celebrating what technical drawing would seek to erase; their very existence as mere representation.

And yet it is clearly evident that in each and all practices of line, that the generic character of line remains resolutely the same throughout each successive encounter. In that, is it not the same line held in relation that enabled the considered design of the concentration camps, built in Germany during the second World War and also that used rather happily in any kindergarten today? This is not to say that these two activities are homologous in any way, but it is to ask if this self-same line contains traces, as in written language, of all previous emplotments?

Are we justified then in speaking of line only in the singular as LINE and not as a multiplicity, particularised depending on each line's mobilisation? For do not all lines share exactly the same attributes, in that differences in length, breadth or contour signify only the method to which line has been successfully drawn out and not a significant difference in kind, in that all lines share the same lineage, the same omnipresent genesis?[4]

4

'…how can the subjective egological evidence of sense become objective and intersubjective? How can it give rise to an ideal and true object, with all the characteristics that we know it to have: omnitemporal validity, universal normativity, intelligibility for "everyone", uprootedness out of all "here and now" factuality, and so forth?' Jacques Derrida, *Edmund Husserl's Origin of Geometry: An Introduction.* trans. John P. Leavey, JR., Lincoln and London: University of Nebraska Press, 1989, p 63

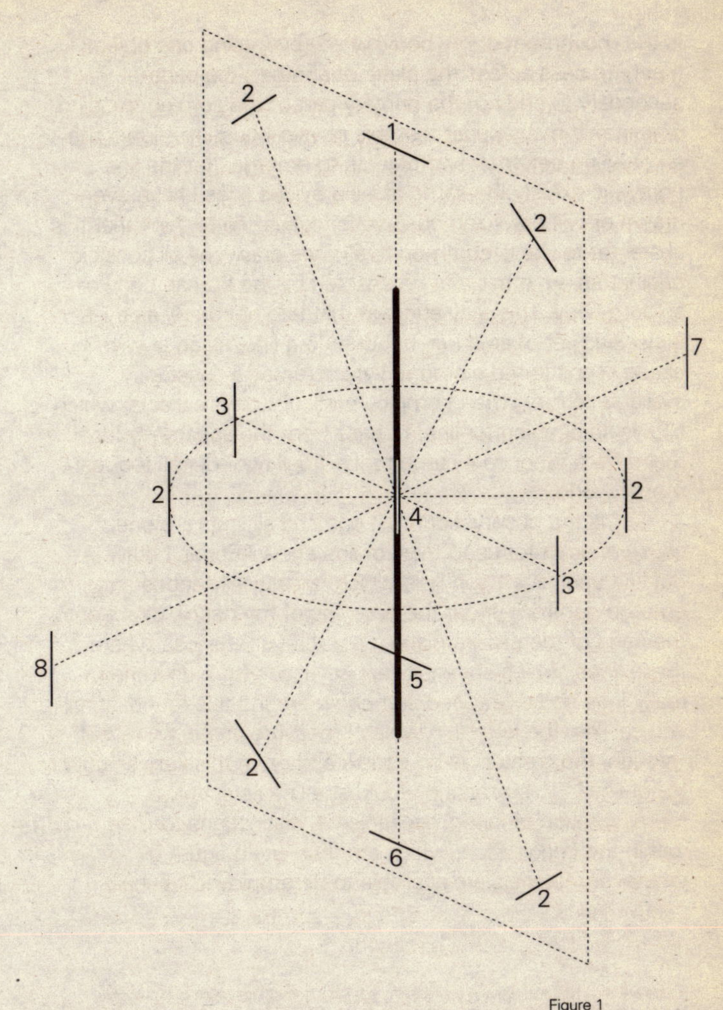

Figure 1
Contra fields
1 Above
2 Oblique
3 Parallel
4 Within
5 Upon
6 Below
7 Behind
8 Infront

Authorship

Is the movement of my body, which by forcing one object;
a pen, to pass across the plane of another; the paper,
secondary to and not the primary part of the coming to being
of a line? It may appear that this physical gesture allows line
an opening between two objects to emerge. Yet the line
I draw, is exactly the same as all previous lines I have ever
drawn or will draw and observation leads me to think that this
character to line is common to all lines drawn by all possible
originators, whether that be enacted by the human body or
an auto-body. This may suggest that I do not draw, as a
conscious act of creation, but draw out line, as an always
already constituted element. Which remains constantly
available to me, when I employ particular physical acts, which
allows an opening for line, to pass from the apparently Ideal
realm from whence it came to the fragility of our all too real
mortal world.

Is the observation, that one and all lines are one,
cause enough for us to think of line anew? For as I draw
out line upon line upon line, which fantastically appears to
emerge out from under the time line of my pencil, direct onto
the pane of the picture plane, I am forever at a loss where
these lines, which so readily appear, issue from. Is it then
really I, as body, wrapped somehow around this foundational
vertical line, the letter I in which I measure and draw myself
through, the creator, as bourgeois author, of this very singular
life of line?[5] This scenario would see line as simply a
representation of inner mechanisms, distinctions formed
within the imagination, which are thus given figure by
whatever materials are available to be employed as
sign vehicles.

5

'There are thus two elements in expression: that inner something which is expressible,
and its outward objectification for others (or possibly for oneself). Any theory of expression,
however complex or subtle a form it may take, inevitably presupposes these two elements
– the whole event of expression is played out between them... The theory of expression
underlying the first trend in philosophy of language is fundamentally untenable. The
experiential, expressible element and its outward objectification are created... out of one
and the same material... there is no such thing as experience outside of the embodiment
of signs... Consequently... It is not experience that organises expression, but the other way
around – expression organises experience.'
   Valentin Nikolaevic Volosinov, *Marxism and The Philosophy of Language*, trans.
Ladislav Matejka and I.R. Titunik, Massachusetts and London: Harvard University Press,
1986, pp 84–85

This may suggest that I choose to talk through line and yet am I really able to choose otherwise? While drawing I do not have the impression of this passage from an inside to an outside. What I experience is a dissolution of the quotidian self, of the subject's self-identity as a discrete object. As any impression I may have previously entertained of being crudely in control of my actions are rendered passive, by an overriding sensation that I do not make lines but am somehow given over to them. Should I then be content as delineator with what may appear as a fallacious picture of self-identity, which would place this author at the centre of what it is to draw a line? When as I look at line, and consider the language of line, its contra fields and how it is mobilised, I am bound also to see another story. Which is not just that of a simple tool used rather cleverly; the grand history of human ingenuity, but also that the practice of drawing, the drawing out of lines endlessly, replays the fictitious, but no less real originary act, when pen incising paper I became the I which actively discriminates.

    It is in this sense that our patent addiction to the drawing of lines, this unquenchable passion for an infinite regress of dividing the real into yet further distinctions, is but a desperate attempt, I would suggest at shoring up a rather shaky picture of the self, as that I which acts, has effects and is clearly 'self evidentially' sovereign. And so this act of self – realisation, which would see the primordial act of drawing the first line, as that which established the human subject as a maker of distinctions, is not without attendant implications.

In that, if we accept that to be an acting subject is to think
by way of distinction, however self-reflexively produced, has
not therefore this adherence, this way of spacing the world,
caused us to succumb to a somewhat 'classical picture' of
our relationship to objects and space generally? Which has
by proceeding to draw ever sharper classificatory boundaries,
what line does so effortlessly, created a tendency to read as
vagaries all that to which line passes over in silence. Could
we then not see line as a nascent material element prior to
human consciousness, through which I think of the world as
constituted by a multiplicity of separations and so fall into a
way of doing, a way of representing, which appears to either
emerge through or be bound to the banal ordinances of line?

   What, though, are the choices available to us if we
proceed against the line, against the consolidated history of
this story? If such a choice exists and I am not yet convinced
it really does, perhaps some light may be found in the search
for a mode of space-less thinking,[6] an oxymoronic territory of
a-temporality, without horizon, without the need to affirm on
the basis of that which bounds.

[6]
'Man without horizon, and not affirming himself on the basis of horizon – in this sense a
being without being, a presence without presence, thus foreign to everything visible and to
everything invisible – he is what comes to me as speech when to speak is not to see. The
Other speaks to me and is only this exigency of speech. And when the Other speaks to me,
speech is the relation of that which remains radically separate, the relation of the third kind
affirming a relation without unity, without equality.' Maurice Blanchot, *The Infinite
Conversation*, trans. Susan Hanson, Minneapolis and London: University of Minnesota Press,
1993, p 69

Autopsy

Looking deep within a line, what do I see? A blank, a void, an abyss, a no-thing? One might wonder why and how a material element which has described and made available so many objects and thoughts, throughout human history, would refuse to show its hand. Imagine then for a moment as Poe once did,[7] of teetering at the edge of a maelstrom, not though to observe a swirling torrent of brine, but so as to stand at the edge of line, to look deep within its matt black heart, to observe within its icy depths a spinning vortex of fragmented shrouds, a mélange of whirling drawn speculations, weird Frankenstein compositions, childish scribbles, impatient graffiti, marooned letters, splintered words, saucy cartoons, mathematical cadavers, strung-out self-portraits, cool diagrams, splenetic lithographs, to mention just a few.

Line though, would appear to have no memory of its actions, I can observe no madly swirling linear soup when I look deep into a line. All I have been able to see, is a complete absence of all of that everything line has helped to bring about. Is this not though all very peculiar? How can an element which has enabled all, nevertheless appear to be so neutral? Is this not but a veil? Should we allow line to exhibit such a mode of self–effacement unchallenged, considering how line, our addiction to line, would inevitably hold so much of our future within its hands? I do not want to suggest here a malicious intent on the part of line, it is just that I certainly cannot be convinced that this absence which is nevertheless so present and enactive could be anything other than neutral. How are we then to talk on line, if we are not just to concentrate on its effects?

7

See Edgar Allan Poe, 'A Descent into the Maelstrom', in, *The Fall of the House of Usher and Other Writings,* (ed.) David Galloway, Penguin, 1986, pp 225–42

The space between objects

Between any two lines resides a space. This space upon and within the picture plane, is a simple result of choosing to see the world as an infinite series of figural limit relations. In that, to be able to read a line 'as a line', we first have to posit the areas where there are no lines; within and upon the picture plane, as a non-object field. A field which, for line to speak, is required to be read as mute and empty of all characteristics, over and above that required to allow line centre stage as the apparent site of all meaning. Similar to discussions around notions of time and space, pictorial space also exhibits characteristics similar to that of three-dimensional experiential space, in that physical space is also variously posited as that without qualities, as infinite and same and without border.

Is the space within the picture always the same? Within any line composition, a set of visually dynamic relationships are evident. Are these relations, though, purely a by-product of the decision to choose to place one line next to another or does the space of relation also (retroactively?) contribute to the meaning of the composition, if the space within the picture plane is not also to be seen as empty, as a site of zero meaning? How then are we to infer qualities upon a zone which would also appear to allude all such attempts at description?

Line and the space between lines appear to hold no inherent meaning. Both have a character, whereby these elements appear to accept all and yet leave no trace upon the dweller therein. How can it be, that line and relation are able to speak, are able to hold meaning, when both also appear to be the embodiment of a radical absence?

Between line and space

Are there not other ways of making distinctions within this world? What though might the alternatives be? To be able to see line as a line, a disarmingly simple distinction has to be made, simply one has to just actively see all, yes all, as line and as not line. This first apparently innocent intuitive step, sifts through the real, ordering the continuum into an infinite collection of figure – ground relationships, of lines and relation, objects and space, contingent and transcendent events. This way of seeing, inevitably creates an ever vaster catalogue of binary oppositions and can be read to have inculcated how we thus phenomenally view time and space generally. To think otherwise, would be to start to break down this primary practice of the rush to distinction, which operating on the level of the 'always already' and hence largely unacknowledged foundation for all theory and yes, all action, is permitted to silently narrate.[8]

If we accept then, for the moment, as currently we possess no theories to suggest otherwise, that both line and relation figure as the antithesis of what we understand by the word materiality. In that both line and space in their respective ways enable signification to proceed only to the extent that each is able to avoid taking on permanently what they signify. How then, can a further condition distinguish itself, between the coquettish game of peekaboo that line is want to play and the grand melodrama of the space of nothingness?

8
'Of what' (is) this is such that it remains invisible though it be the fundamental condition of the visible, such that it be unable to be posed though it be the condition for all posing, such that it not be produced, yet be the condition for all production, such that it have no origin but be the originary itself.' Luce Irigarary, *The Forgetting of Air in Martin Heidegger*, London: The Athlone Press, 1999, p 4

A third condition may exist though, for between any two
things or concepts, two edges are inevitably created. As for
distinctions between things generally to arise, a border
condition is required within the everyday tactics of discourse,
to be neither this nor that, but only that which allows
distinctions to pass. We can agree, that for all things or
concepts to exist, as stable unitary (working) ideas, some
sense of edge (however ambivalent) is certainly required. And
so, the two edges of line and relation inevitably infer a third
condition, located somewhere between them. The character
of this condition is neither that of a line nor a relation, but
that of a no-man's-land. A territory outside of the law of
distinction. And if you will permit me a little visual trickery in
pushing the words space and line together, to produce the
word spine, we could come to name and then eventually to
see, through this minor bricolage, this illusive third relation,
which exactly is situated between line and space.

Could a super-transcendent space, a spatiality
understood outside of a system of oppositions really be said
to exist outside of the space of the imagination? Or does it
only have a life between the letters and white spaces on this
page and not out there… in the world? If you peer closely
enough though, I really wonder, can you see anything? And
if you do, what would a drawing of such a zone look like?
Indeed is line able to capture that which falls outside of
the line–space relation? Which, as neither friend nor foe,
would appear to exist as a permanent stranger to our
strict delineation's.

Conclusion

Within these few lines, I have tried to sketch out some questions regarding how we could start to think line anew and further, how such readings need to be cognizant of, that by concentrating on line alone (in whatever manifestation) as the primary signifier within a composition, that this effectively omits how the trio *line – spine – relation* are inculcated within the heart of the production of what we understand as – the visual.

To summarise then, line can either be seen simply as produced by the mechanics, the anatomy of perception, what the mind and eyes allow us to perceive phenomenally. This would allow us to see vision as mercilessly separating the continuum into an infinite regress of discrete elements, which are evaluated and so distinguished, both by simple comparison, a natural science of perception and also by and within belief. Here the real prior to vision, can be imagined, as similar in appearance to a Rorschach test, in the sense that the act of producing this world, is wholly dependent on our choosing to read a general 'drifting inhabitation' of blots, as a series of speaking figural distinctions.[9] Or we may choose to see line as an already existent element similar in the way we choose to read matter generally, as prior to human history and the dawning of consciousness. In this respect, we may like to enquire, if line exhibits a particular panchronic regularity, upon and within the picture plane, does this character of line, as a self–regulating autonomous element, discipline in any way.

Happily though this tension around who and what is drawing a line dissipates during the act of drawing. As by each sweep of my arm, as line upon line is successively drawn out, I gradually enter, as if in a dream, a site of pure potentiality.

10
See Hilary Lawson, *Closure, A Story of Everything*, London and New York: Routledge, 2001

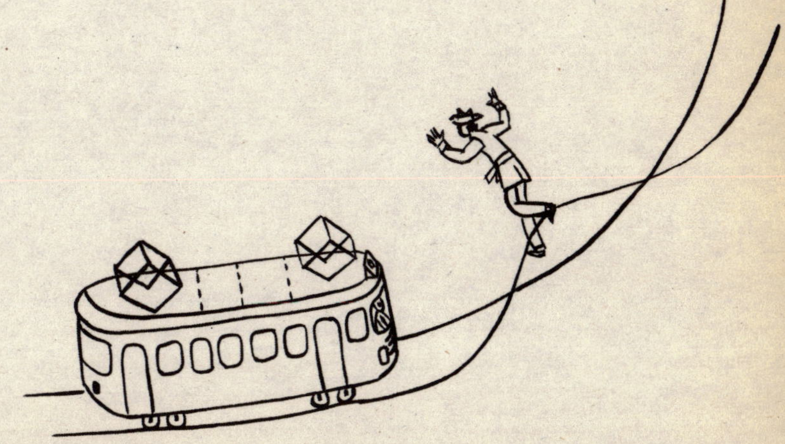

Dotted lines

Lodged in an architectural archive at the bottom of the world,[1] Joshua Kirby's 1755 book, *Perspective of Architecture: a work entirely new…* announces that 'All those lines that are boundaries to the several parts of Architecture, are either straight or circular; and therefore those two different kinds of lines variously applied, may be said to constitute the principal parts of the order.'[2] The lines that construct the fine drawings and text are certain and containing; the curvature of the earth is framed, as is the path of progress.

In this and many subsequent manuals or instructional accounts of architecture the drawing of lines – which is also the construction of the limits of the architectural object – is subject to technical and anecdotal regulation. The line is not only the primary mode of drawing technique, but is also the primary structuring device within the design process. Linearity, characteristic of Western thought, pervades the discipline despite architecture's engagement with curvilinear space and baroque effects. The line is characteristically continuous, even and straight.

However, within the straightness of the line, (perhaps because of the power of its thrust – its flight and friction), certain other conditions arise. Catherine Ingraham has probed the materiality of abstract geometry arguing that linearity does not stay cleanly in the world of ideal geometry[3] and also the writer Paul Carter has unfurled the arabesques caused by the meeting of line and other. 'It is the linear thrust itself, as it penetrates the 'other', that creates the counter patterns rolling back from the lip of the hole.'[4]

Despite Kirby's restrictions on the nature of lines that were to be operative in architecture the drawings in his volume also deploy another condition of the line. Dotted and dashed lines appear in his fine engravings to mark invisible

[1]
Architecture Archive, University of Auckland, Auckland, New Zealand

[2]
Joshua Kirby, *The Perspective of Architecture: A Work Entirely New, deduced from the principles of Dr Brook Taylor, and performed by two rules only of universal application, begun by command of his present Majesty when Prince of Wales*, London, 1755

[3]
Catherine Ingraham, 'Initial Proprieties: Architecture and the Space of the Line', in, *Sexuality and Space*, (ed.) Beatriz Colomina, Princeton: Princeton Architectural Press, 1992, pp 254–71

[4]
Paul Carter, *The Lie of the Land*, London and Boston: Faber & Faber, 1996, p 298

centrelines and to indicate movement necessary to the
construction of figures. Dotted lines, tracing unseen
geometries, have been allowed into the discipline to deal with
the invisible, the implied and the mobile. Like the matter and
arabesques of linearity, dots and dashes, caught firmly within
the straight line, also serve to gently critique its rigid nature.
Hidden and phantom conditions are productive weaknesses
within the disciplinary practices of the architectural drawing.[5]
Wang, in his 1996 manual on the practices of architectural
drawing, (a genre generally committed to clarity and
straightforwardness) reveals a world in which the self-evident
presence of the plan is frequently undercut by a dotted line.
'Dotted or short-dashed lines represent unseen edges of an
object. Continuous lines represent the visible edges. Short-
dashed lines in general represent hidden or unseen objects
in front of or below the observer. In plan drawings, these lines
are often used to indicate objects underground. In sections
and elevations, they are often used to indicate the location
of objects behind any opaque planes.'[6]

    Beneath the resolution and self-sufficiency of the plan
is a zone in which unseen bodies force alteration to the
everyday, planar surfaces of architecture. Dotted lines indicate
a partial condition of unseen physical presence as it exudes or
imprints on the matter before the viewer. These removed
forces become outlined on the opaque surfaces of
architecture, which are consequently rendered as permeable.
Leaking through, the 'unseen' conditions start to materialise,
the surface shifts towards transparency.

    Not only unseen things but also phantom conditions
are marked into architectural drawings. When broken lines
take the form of a series of long dashes Patten & Rogness
in their instructional volume refer to them as 'phantom lines'.[7]

[5] W. Abbott & W. Millar, *Building Drawing with Notes on Building Construction*, London,
Glasgow, Bombay: Blackie and Son Limited, 1926, p 4

[6] Thomas C. Wang, *Plan and Section Drawing* (2nd edition), NY: Van Nostrand Reinhold,
1996, p 41

[7] L.M. Patten & M.L Rogness, *Architectural Drawing* (revised edition), Dubuque, Iowa:
Wm. C. Brown Co. Publishers, 1968, pp 2–3

They are utilised in such situations as a particular, specific detail is drawn in a generalised structural condition. The traditional, hierarchical arrangements in which structure may be seen to take precedence over detail become undone by a structure rendered as partial, dissolving and impermanent with a long dashed line.

Dots and dashes in architectural drawings often signify a repressed spatial movement as Porter and Goodman indicate in their 1985 drawing manual: 'The dashed or broken line represents the third category. This line has an important function in orthographics because it represents a convention of depth. For instance, lines that are broken using short dashes function as 'hidden lines' and signify objects that occur behind the plane of the drawing. Conversely, long-dashed lines signify objects that occur forward of the plane, ie, between the viewer and the cut.'[8]

If the plan has been seen as a cut that reveals everything at once, on one plane, dotted and dashed lines indicate the necessity of reading the vertical effects from above and below onto that plane. Dotted lines induce the viewer to shift between underground and surface condition and back again. The 'conventions of depth' that Porter and Goodman identify point to a past and future occupation of the plan condition and the movement that inevitably takes place between.

Dotted lines also record the movements of the shaping of architectural forms and figures. Joshua Kirby's dotted lines rotate the eye and hand of viewer and maker through the spatial fabrications of the orders. Dotted lines activate the seemingly closed contours of his figures suggesting that movement could bring about other formal possibilities. With their shimmering lack of completion and their variable speeds (dots are surely slow compared to the headlong rush of a dash) dotted and dashed lines suggest that the making of architecture is always a mobile speculation.

8
Tom Porter and Sue Goodman, *Manual of Graphic Techniques for Architects, Graphic Designers & Artists* (vol 4), New York: Charles Scribners and Sons, 1985, p 10

Such speculative tendencies in broken lines are both
mobilised and resisted in their deployment as boundary lines.
Boundaries that attempt to insist on closure and containment.
are often constructed in architectural drawings with a series
of dots and dashes. Long – short – short – long – intermittent
gestures of ownership and control but the inherent
permeability of such lines suggests that the boundary might
be seen as negotiable. In architectural drawings dotted lines,
representing approximate borderlines or approximate
conjunctions for which there may not yet be full agreement,
also indicate sites of contention.

Signalling the presence and absence of matter dotted
and dashed lines have within them the possibility of complete
rupture; reading the darkness of ink or graphite as depth, as
perforation, dots mark a line of separation. As a warning of
frailty and the construction of weakness, the partial and
intermittent nature of the dotted lines is found by Kasha
Linville to be an underlying condition of the straight line.

She discovers this in Agnes Martin's pencil lines that
grid her watercolours: 'her line is sharp… Sometimes its own
shadow softens it… Most often her line respects the canvas
grain, skimming its surface without filling the low places in
the fabric so it becomes almost a dotted or broken line at
close range.'[9] Even ideal geometry is, in the end, molecular,
catching on the surface in a pulse between the physical
and cerebral.

The flickering solid/void, on/off pattern of the dotted
line suggests the structuring of digital drawings. Digital
drawings, like dotted lines, deal with the imaginary, the
speculative and the partial and are committed to the
unfinished and the mobile. Materiality becomes intermittent
or dispersed in both dashed lines and digital drawings and
matter is reduced to component level; on/off, matter/void,
current-inducing oscillation. Electrical pulses that drive digital
constructions are activated in orthographic drawings with the
spatial connections and ruptures of dotted and dashed lines.

9
Kasha Linville, in, Rosalind Krauss, *Bachelors*, Cambridge, Mass: October, MIT Press,
1999, p 79

The on/off digital patterning of dots and dashes suggests that these lines, as in Ingraham's analysis, are coded with bodily rhythms that complicate (bloodless) ideal geometry as the only grounds for architectural making. Rosalind Krauss, writing on a piece by Duchamp suggests that 'the oscillation figured in the work through the back-and-forth of its rhythmic arc operates as a temporal analogue to the shifting undecidability of its definition of male and female.'[10] On/off, residual matter/gap, dotted lines trace bodily cycles of pleasure into architecture. A beat induced, not only in the on/off pulse, but also in an approximate flickering shift between drawings and built architecture, potential and completion.

Broken lines also have a desire for completion; join-the-dots and discover meaning. Restoration and reconstruction drawings often use the dotted line to imagine perfection and restore unity to the damaged or fragmentary. Such drawings are a speculation concerning the past in the present and acknowledge an alternative to continuous, linear accounts of time. Attempts to navigate time with dotted lines is to formally step in and out of the present, past and future.

Dotted and dashed lines suggest the fabrication of narratives. Three dots in a line at the end of a sentence invite speculation on the next event leaving the uncertainty of the dotted line trailing out of the story; a refusal of completion and an invitation to continue. As Nigel Lewis puts it: 'a minute attention to spottedness in things, (is) an attention so marked that one sometimes has the impression of an obsessively pointilliste word painter at work behind the scenes. This is a world required to read alterations in surface appearance for tiny signs of danger, divine displeasure, the malign influence of the stars: the eruption on faces which might mean the plague…'[11]

10
Rosalind Krauss, 'The Im/pulse to See', in, *Vision and Visuality,* (ed.) by Hal Foster, Dia Art Foundation, Seattle: Bay Press, 1988, p 63
11
Nigel Lewis, *The Book of Babel: Words and the Way we see Things,* London: Penguin Books, 1994, p 49

In his *Ten Books on Architecture*, Vitruvius looked to the stars, intermittent dots of light, 'visible or invisible according to fixed times', and found linear designs; the constellations Archer, Scorpion and Balance.[12] He traced the movements of the figures and the consequent patterns of sun and moonlight, and fitted his account of architecture into a wider world. Those dots of light in a black sky, that Vitruvius saw were also navigational aids for the first inhabitants of South Pacific islands. They followed the lines and patterns of stars from island to island. Islands that came to be represented on European maps in the eighteenth century as small dots in a vast ocean.[13]

The lines of the European explorers, marked on the charts from anchor point to anchor point with small dots, encountered, across the permeable boundary of the foaming shore, suggest a new sort of architecture. Architecture in the Pacific is traditionally structured through systems of intermittent linearity, lines of weft and warp woven together. Systems of weaving that depend upon the appearance and disappearance of material lines as they construct surface. Weaving can be seen as a technology of dotted lines as it builds gaps, as well as matter, into architecture.

As Marco Frascari has pointed out: '[a]ll 'lines' used in other crafts requiring metis [cunning intelligence] derive from the lines used in a loom. The tracing on the ground at a construction site shows clearly the textile origin of construction. The plan of a future building is marked by the tracing lines (pulled between the battered boards), which together resemble a huge horizontal loom. This shows that a plan of an edifice is woven, like fishing or hunting nets.'[14]

[12]
Vitruvius, *Ten Books of Architecture*, trans. M. M. Morgan, New York: Dover Publications Inc, 1960, p 258

[13]
The Shorter Oxford Dictionary (1973) gives as a definition of dot, 'A small island... represented in the general chart... only by A.D 1748'

[14]
Marco Frascari, 'The Compass and the Crafty Art of Architecture', *Modulus* 22, 1991, p 7

Watching for the critical opening gap, the woof line surfaces and dives into the rising and falling path of the warp line constructing together a dazzling surface.[15] The simple singularity of the straight vector is replaced by a surface construction that leaves room for criss-crossing, back-tracking. As Carter points out, such tracking, marked like a sequence of footfalls across ground, is not conceived of in terms of progress or efficiency but is instead another sort of linearity, like a dotted line, sometimes over and above itself, composed of 'potential crossroads', responsive to circumstantial contingencies.

Through the gaps in the woven wall come sounds, spacing, breath... 'For neat work the draughtsman must be prepared to take pains and do his dotted lines without mechanical aid. It is a help, when doing a dash line of any length, to count mentally 1–2–3–4– 1–2–3–4–5 etc, keeping time with the pen.'[16] Dotted line architecture, woven as a network is premised on the rise and fall of bodily cycles; it is lightly fabricated and disinterested in permanence. In the darkness of the woven interior points of light construct architectural effects recalled in the gleaming lights that appear out of the black void of the computer screen. The persistence and pleasures of these dotted lines are rhythmically patterned into the flickering, mobile constructions of new architectural space, Pacific space.

[15] 'And besides, while it may be true that the weaver has to time the passage of the arrow-headed shuttle with the woof to ensure it finds the warp's gap, the critical moment originates outside, and the successful weaver is he who aligns himself completely with its movement.' Paul Carter, *The Lie of the Land*, London and Boston: Faber & Faber, 1996, p 320

[16] W. H. Smith, *A Guide to Draughtsmanship*, London: E. & F. N. Spon, 1943, p 29

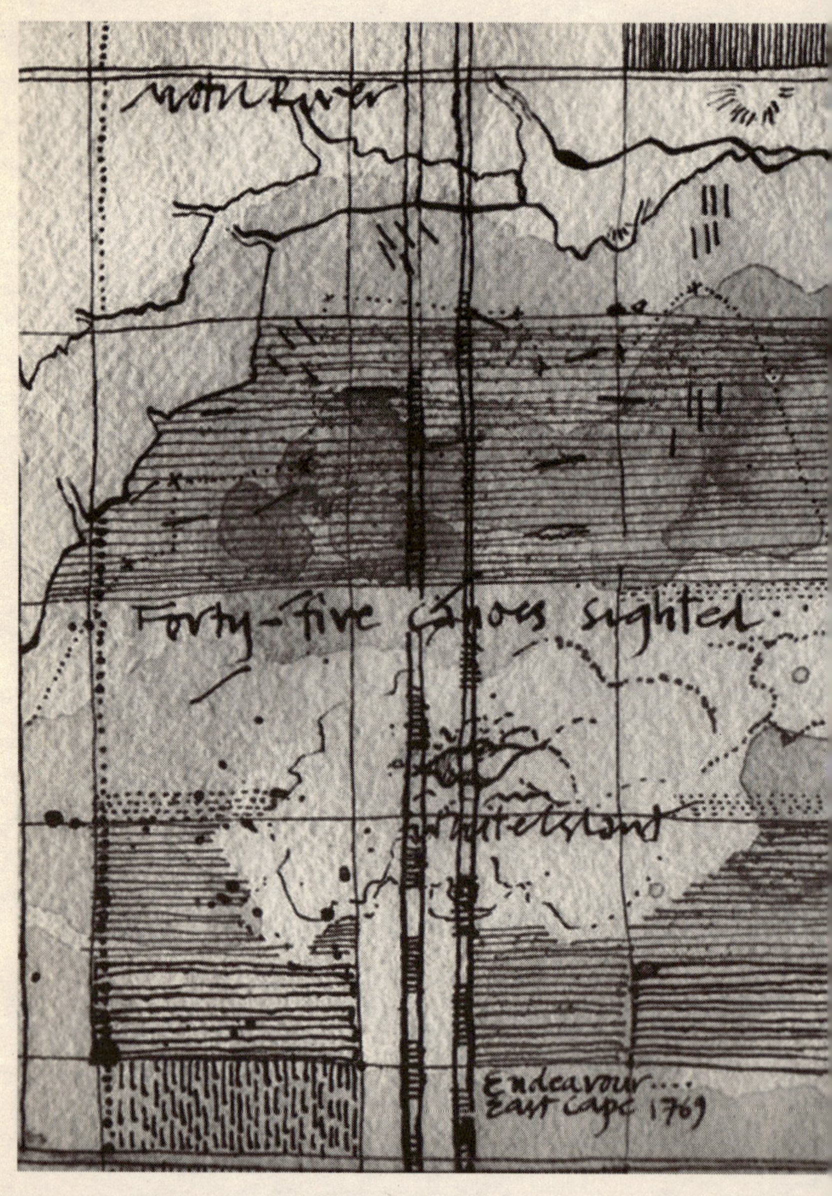
North River
Forty-five canoes sighted
White Island
Endeavour....
East Cape 1769

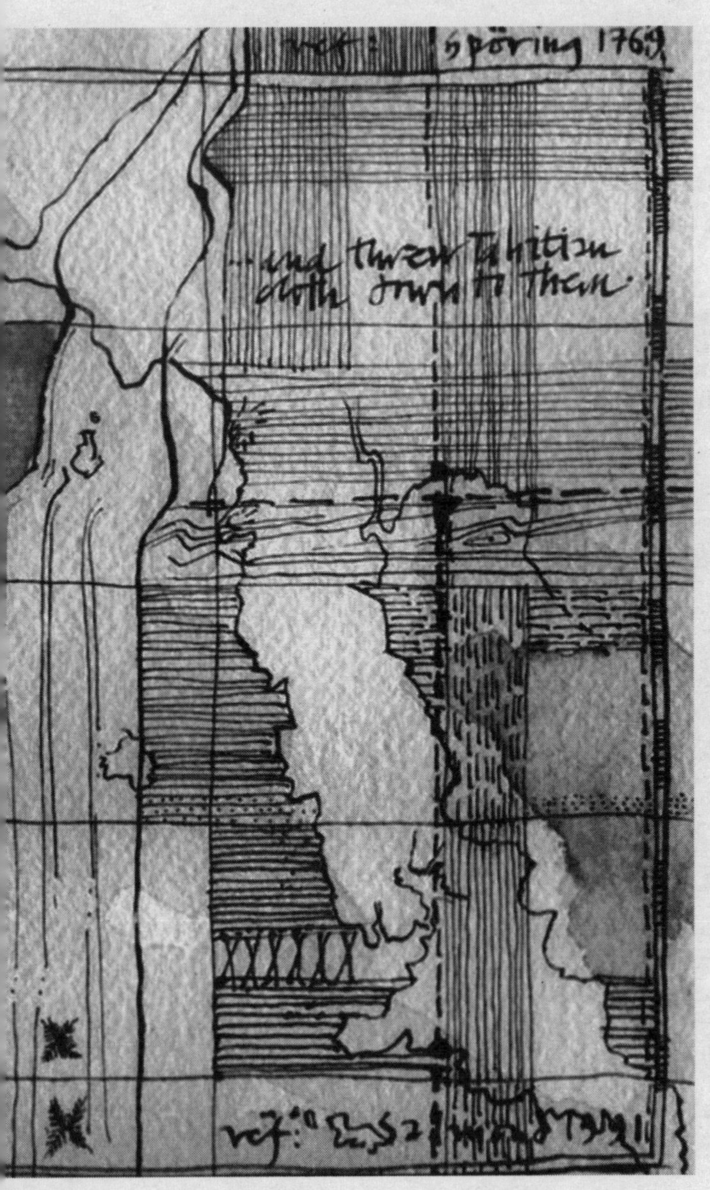

Spöring 1769
...and twenty Tahitian
cloth down to them.

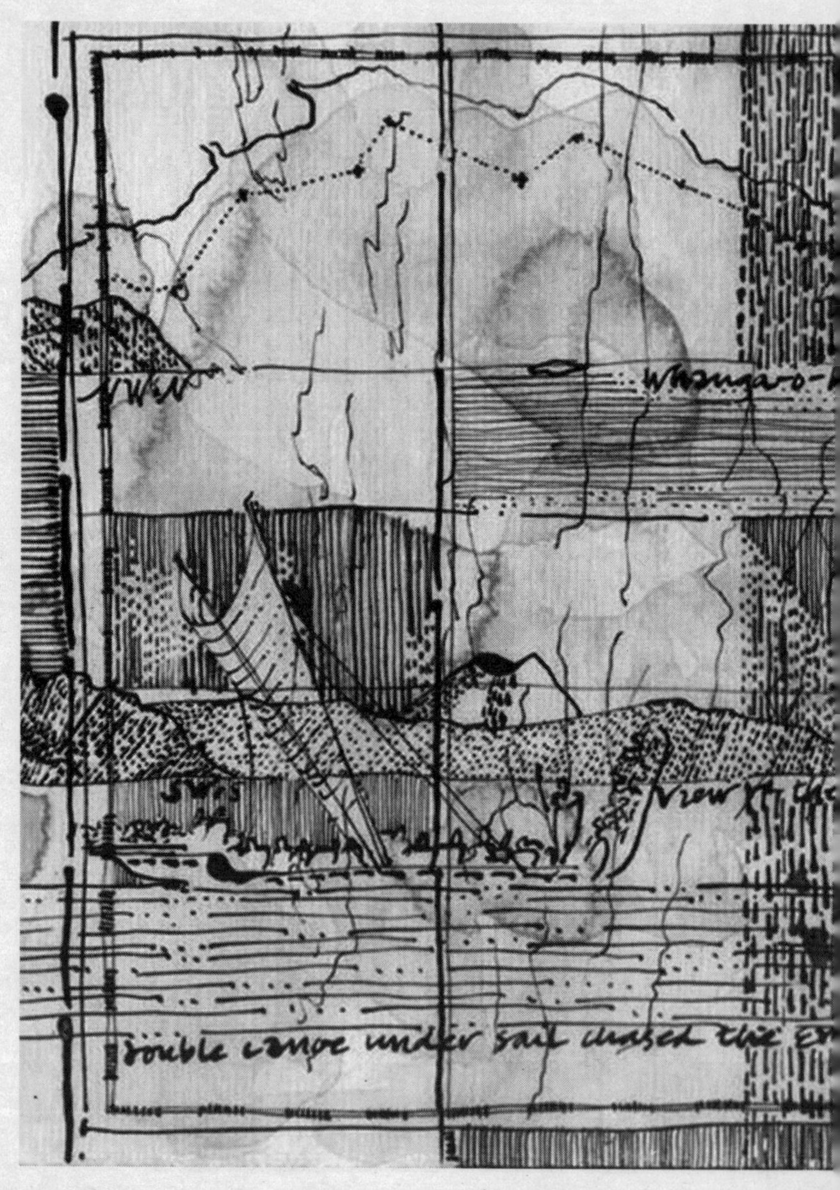

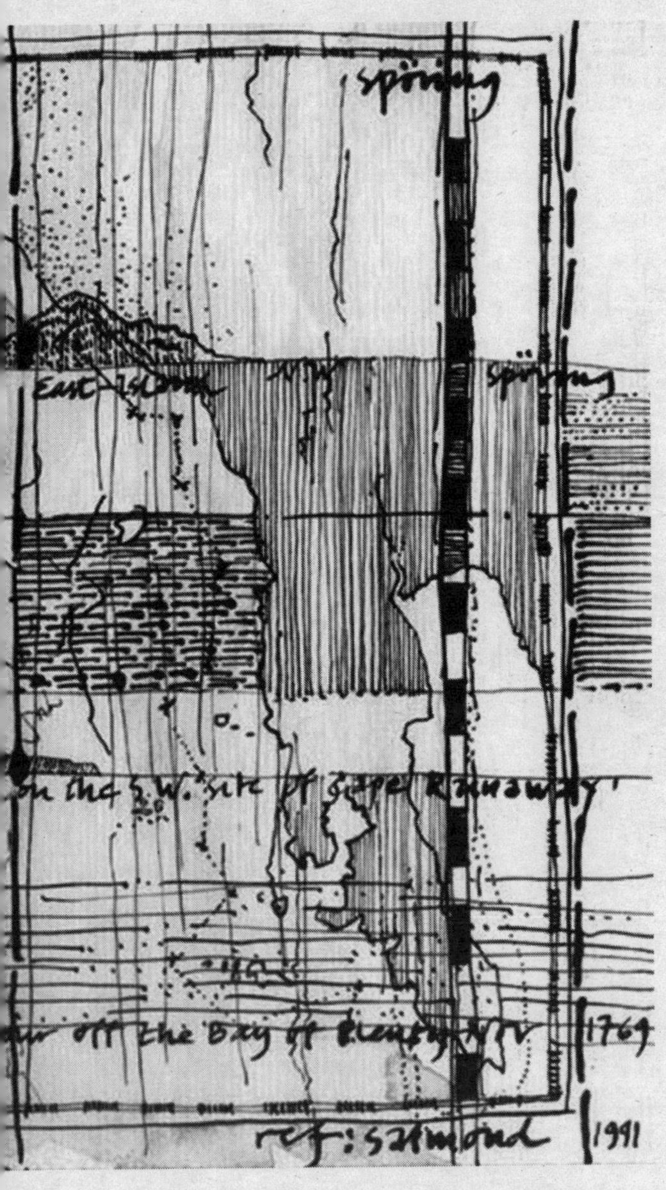
spring
spring
East
1769
1991

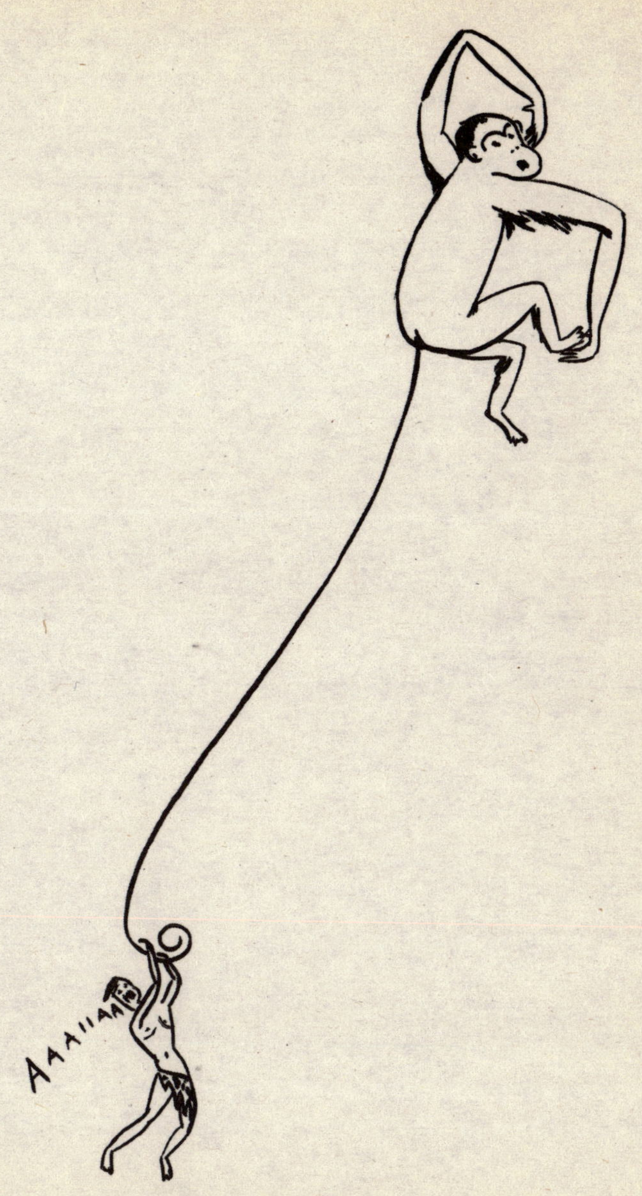
AAAIIAA

Adolf Loos is familiar to us today as historically the first enemy
of ornament. The pristine severity of his white cubes, the bold
linkage of rationality with monumentality, and the renunciation
of the suffocating, portentous ornamentation of his time made
him one of the most important founding fathers of the modern.
Some of Loos's unrealised designs, however, stand
out from this canon of simplicity. The house designed for
Josephine Baker, 1927, (see linear facade study, figure 1) or the
columnar skyscraper for the Chicago Tribune, 1922 also display
another aspect that would again be focused on in the
postmodern era. Can a certain playfulness, or even a flirtation
with ornamentation, be discerned in these designs? Some
scholars have implied as much, which raises the question of
how Loos dealt in his architectural work with the aesthetic
consequences of his radical theory. In this regard, I find
especially noteworthy his treatment of line, through which,
as I hope to demonstrate, Loos attempted to expel the erotic.
It was with strong language, within his 1908 moral
theory of culture, that Loos condemned ornamentation as a
crime. For Loos, ornaments must vanish from useful objects
as they were 'pathological symptoms' hindering humanity in
its cultural development, and as such are retrograde signs of
'wasted productive energy', causing harm to the national
economy. For Loos, the development of art and commerce is
seen to be interdependent with public hygiene. Thus it was
that he considered the great accomplishment of modern man
to be such: '…that ornament no longer incited feelings of lust,
to the extent that a tattooed face, unlike among the Papuans,
did not increase the aesthetic feeling, but diminished it.'[1]
In this context, contemporary feminist scholarship has
focused primarily on Loos's characteristic equation of women
with primitives and criminals. For primitives, so Loos claimed,
ornament represented the beginnings of art, what he also
described as the 'babble of painting':

1

Adolf Loos, 'Ornament und Verbrechen', in, *Theorien der Gestaltung*, (eds.) Volker Fischer
& Anne Hamilton, Frankfurt: Verlag Form, 1999, p 115

Figure 1
Josephine Baker
house. All linear
facade studies by
Gordon Shrigley

'The Papuan tattoos his skin, his boat, his rudder, in short, everything accessible to him. He is no criminal. The modern human who tattoos himself is a criminal or a degenerate. There are prisons in which eighty percent of the inmates bear tattoos.'[2]

Thus, a criminal is only one who attempts to apply ornament within modern society. Loos complained of his contemporaries that 'the addiction to ornament is officially recognised and subsidised with public funds.'[3] Along with past cultural epochs, which, in accordance with the aesthetic sense innate to them, did not yet know how to do without ornament, for Loos it is particularly women who always retain an affinity to ornamentation.[4] Needing as a woman did to impress men with her toilette, ornament would 'live eternally' in the service of woman. This hopeless case was the result of the unavoidable eroticism of the female: 'The ornament of the female represents fundamentally that of the savage; it has erotic meaning.'[5]

2
Adolf Loos, *Ornament und Verbrechen*, ibid, p 114. Stephan Oettermann has shown that already before 1900, criminological-anthropological research had concluded that the tattooed, ie those who applied ornament even to their own bodies, were disproportionately likely to commit crimes. See his *Zeichen auf der Haut: Die Geschichte der Tätowierung*, Frankfurt am Main: Europa, 1985

3
Adolf Loos, *Ornament und Verbrechen*, ibid, p 116

4
Loos assumed that a creator exercised no influence on cultural development, but was instead subject to a zeitgeist forcing him to create in the style fitting to his time, as he wrote in his article 'Kulturentartung' (1908): 'We do not sit the way we do because a carpenter has constructed the chair in a certain way; rather, the carpenter builds the chair this way because this is how we wish to sit.' Cited in Fischer and Hamilton (eds.), ibid, p 112

5
Adolf Loos, 'Ornament und Erziehung', in, *Wohnungskultur, Monatszeitschrift für Industrielle Kunst*, 1924/1925. Cited in Christina Threuter, 'Ausgerechnet Bananen: Die Ornamentfrage bei Adolf Loos', in, *Um-Ordnung: Angewandte Kunst und Geschlecht in der Moderne, (eds.)* Cordula Bischoff and Christina Threuter (ed.) Marburg: Jonas, 1999, p 108

Christina Threuter has described at length how Loos's stigmatisation of ornament as a degenerate, criminal and, especially, compulsive element, as well as its ascription to the female, coincided with the prevailing discourse in medical and psychoanalytic circles around 1900.[6] Between misogyny and demonisation, according to Threuter, and influenced by Darwin's evolutionary theory, the discussion culminated in the question of the intellectual and biological inferiority of women. In this analysis, the Art Nouveau image of the female simply reflects the neurotic sexual anxiety typical of the age. Threuter points to the interesting case of Loos's project for Josephine Baker. As she sees it, the Baker house, with its stripe spreading across the facade, displays an ornament within which the architect denies his own theory. This conundrum may be explained by interpreting the house for Baker, who as an Afro-American revue star and symbol of the exotic represented the living-out of sexual fantasies, as follows: 'It represents in Loos's reading the image of the female and that of the primitive. The formation of the house's facade is sexualised and connoted in the sense of an unrestrained libidinousness: Loos tattooed the house, he clothed it in erotic urges, and it represents in accordance with his evolutionistic model of development a lack of culture amidst the civilised culture.'[7]

This explanation seems at first logical, but reveals itself to be problematic in two respects: First, it is unclear whether Loos even considered stripes as ornamental. I believe that a closer examination of the specific application of stripes and lines in Loos's designs can only lead to the conclusion that he saw these not as ornament, but as a successful alternative thereto. Secondly, Loos's social engagement belied his statement mentioned above that women would remain eternally bound to ornamentation. If Loos is to be charged with self-contradiction, then it is here, and only here.

6
See Threuter, ibid, p 108. In this framework, important reference texts include Otto Weiningers, *Geschlecht und Charakter* (1908), Sigmund Freud, *Drei Abhandlungen zur Sexualtheorie* (1905), and Karl Kraus, *Sittlichkeit und Kriminalität* (1908)

7
See Threuter, ibid, p 112

In no way did Loos attempt to reinforce the idea of the
eternally erotic and therefore criminal woman; on the contrary,
he called for the 'education of the woman', to whom, along
with the condemnation mentioned above, he also attributed
unusual creative and developmental powers. Thus, for
example, apart from praising his first wife, the actress Lina
Obertimpfler, as a seer and visionary, he also maintained a lively
connection with the Vienna Ladies' Club, whose new rooms
he designed and furnished in 1902.[8]

The Ladies club rooms, similar to the bedroom
designed for his wife Lina, published in 1903, function as
sacred stages on which woman is paid homage. The rational,
yet atmospheric design is apparently the artist's attempt to
contribute to woman's cultural development. For Loos, though,
the future of the female demands the total eradication of her
previous native character – her ur-female principles must be
overcome before she can take her place alongside man:
'That which is noble in woman knows but one longing:
to hold her own against the big, strong man. Currently, this
longing can only be fulfilled when the woman wins the love
of the man. But we are moving into a new and greater era.
No longer the appeal to sensuality, but the economic
independence earned by work will bring about equality with
the male. A woman's value, or lack thereof, will not rise or
fall with changes in sensuality. Then, the effect of satin and
silk, flowers and ribbons, feathers and colours will fail.
They will vanish.'[9]

[8]
For more on this, see Roland L. Schachel, 'Aufgaben einer Loos Biographie', in, *Adolf Loos*,
(ed.) Graphische Sammlung Albertina, Vienna: 1989, pp 15–40

[9]
Adolf Loos, 'Damenmode': Dokumente der Frau, Vienna: 1902. Cited here after Burkhard
Rukschcio and Roland Schachel, *Adolf Loos: Leben und Werk*. Salzburg, Vienna: Residenz-
Verlag, 1982, p 79

It is clear that, in Loos's eyes, the emancipation of the female can proceed only through the cleansing of herself of all aspects of erotic play and sensuality. The complete equality for which he aimed could only be achieved by a rationalisation of her nature, which would place her in the economy of the male.

With this in mind, let us return again to Loos's design for Josephine Baker (figure 1). Christina Threuter has described the design's stripe as an ornamental allusion to the star's eroticism. Beyond the objection that Loos sought to suppress, not to bolster the eroticisation of the woman, this interpretation is also problematic given that stripes appear as the characteristic design element in several of his other projects. It thus seems to me that Loos's work with stripes, with straight lines in parallel, followed an aesthetic strategy of which, as a completely ornament-free design solution, he could make successful use.

Let us more closely examine the phenomenon of Loos's stripes: the vertically oriented stripe of the Chicago Tribune Column may be seen as the antithesis of the Baker house's horizontal stripe. Loos designed the 120-metre Doric column in response to a contest for a new office building for the newspaper. He interpreted the word 'column' as a metaphor for both newspaper column and statue of the free world. The body of the tower rises 40 storeys, fluted with 28 vertical channels housing the windows. The entire building was to be clad in black, polished granite. Indeed, the building contains not a single bent or broken line. The capital of the column is kept as plain as possible, the polished stone allows for no unevenness that might appear as waves or bulges; the picture is dominated accordingly by the vertical orientation of the flutes, which resemble stripes.

Ornament and hysteria:
How Adolf Loos exorcised the erotic play of line

For his perhaps most famous work, the building on
Michaelerplatz, Vienna (1909–11), Loos initially prepared
several different designs for a facade. He was apparently
unsure whether the radical nakedness of the final design as
eventually carried out would meet with success, and so he
prepared a version with stripes. This design for the facade
shows a horizontal banding of the upper storeys through
narrow wavy meandering lines. Such horizontal banding was
entirely typical of Loos; in addition to his design for Baker,
he also used it on the war ministry design (Vienna) and the
projected hotel on Friedrichstrasse (Berlin).[10]
    The stripe motif surfaces most frequently in Loos's
interior design projects. For the purposes of our investigation,
the rooms designed for women as discussed above bear
special significance. The bedroom for Loos's wife features
half-height curtains of white batiste rayée encircling the entire
room, dividing it horizontally into two bands. The pleats of the
curtains introduce vertical stripes into the room, and the fabric
itself is also finely striped. The stripe design of the curtains
serves here to hide the clothes cupboards behind, while the
absence of any other furniture save bed and toilette table
heightens the stage-like effect of the bed as a sacred alter.
    Loos did not hesitate to use this design principle
for the walls of both public and private spaces, as his interior
for the Vienna Ladies' Club demonstrates. Contemporary
reviews praised its elegance and tasteful lighting,
'a comfortable clubhouse in the best English and American
tradition,' noting that 'everywhere have been chosen
pleasing, agreeable shapes and colours that do not insult
the eye.'[11] Photographs of the space again show the
conspicuous vertical stripes of the wall covering, which
Loos also intended as an exhibition space. A horizontal band
approximately 70 cm wide and meant for the display of
pictures runs around the room at eye level.

[10]
See Burkhard Rukschcio and Roland Schachel, ibid, p 149
[11]
Cited here after Burkhard Rukschcio and Roland Schachel, ibid, p 71

To return to the facade, let us briefly examine the Villa
Spanner near Gumpoldskirchen, Lower Austria 1923, (see
linear facade study, figure 2). Here, too, attention is drawn to
the vertical lines or stripes that form the central element of
the design. The interpretation of the Baker house and its
horizontal stripe as an erotic allusion must be rejected in the
face of this building, a counterpart not designed for a female
client. The zig-zag pattern of the window shutters is the most
noticeable design element of the facade (figure 3). Here, the
course of the line or stripe is begun at a diagonal, interrupted,
then continued in the other diagonal. This arrangement of
linear elements would, of course, be nothing out of the
ordinary, but seen from the background of Loos's utter
rejection of ornament, it becomes an aesthetic position – for
is such a lightning bolt zig-zag not undoubtedly an ornament?
But, once again, Loos need not contradict himself, if one
but narrows down his definition of ornament.

Loos, in one possible resolution of the apparent
contradiction, was attempting to educate the line of the
ornament to a state of non-ornamentality, through connecting
the two points of a line in as rational a manner as possible:
without a flourish, meander or curve. For Loos, the only
acceptable line was the straight line, or multiple lines in
parallel. An ornament, one might define with Loos, is created
by the curving of a line; the straight line may be seen as
unerotic, and therefore free of ornament. In fact, the
banishing of the erotic in favour of the economic comprises
a cornerstone of this definition: The bent or otherwise curved
line represents the 'wasting of productive energy' and thus
a sin against the economy. The zig-zag line is indeed on the
threshold of ornament; however, its perfectly straight lines
connect the points in as directly a manner as possible,
allowing the zig-zag to pass as rationally and economically
acceptable.

Figure 2
Villa Spanner linear
facade study

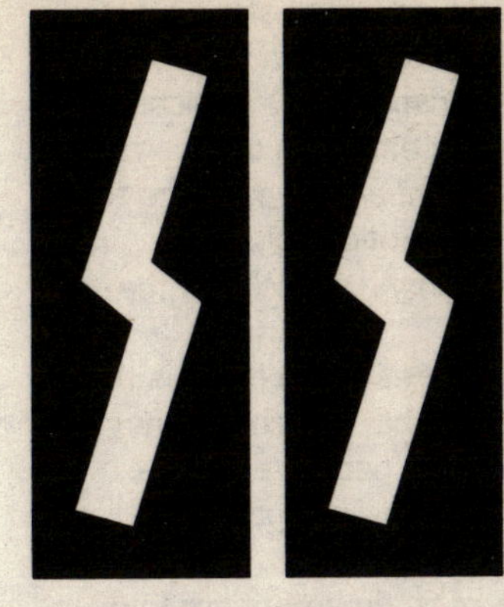

Figure 3
Villa Spanner, zig-zag
window shutter study

To carry this argumentation a step further: the stripe created
by two straight and parallel lines can be seen in Loos's work
as a successful antithesis to the Christian cross, which he
saw as the precursor of the insistent eroticism of ornament.
Loos explained his theory in *Ornament and Crime*: 'The first
ornament to be born, the cross, had erotic origins…
A horizontal line: the reclining woman. A vertical line: the
man penetrating her.'[12] (figure 4)

The intersection of the two lines in the cross is the
most radical form in which two lines may 'touch', as they
penetrate one another. However, Loos had to recognise even
their precursors, ie curved, hence gradually approaching lines,
as erotic and therefore uneconomic ornaments.

What has the curved line of an ornament got to do
with gender? The iconography of the bent line, as has been
argued before, was closely linked in Art Nouveau with
research into hysteria.[13] The diagnosis of hysteria was
interpreted as gender-specific around 1900 and, as a
phenomenon occurring in such a short and clearly
demarcated span of time, received unprecedented media
attention in photographs of the era.[14] In this context, an
especially vivid image was provided by what Jean-Martin
Charcot described as the 'arc de cercle', the hysterical arch
or circle – an image, not coincidentally, one may see in Art
Nouveau representations of the female body. Charcot
defines this body arch as follows:

[12]
Adolf Loos, *Ornament und Verbrechen*, ibid, p 114
[13]
See the two figures 'Die Salpêtrière ikonographiert ihre Hysterie' & 'Der Jugendstil
ikonographiert seine Hysterie', in, Friedrich Kittler, *Grammophon, Film, Typewriter*, Berlin:
Brinkmann und Bose, 1986, pp 212 – 17
[14]
See Friedrich Kittler, ibid, and Georges Didi-Hubermann, *Erfindung der Hysterie – die
photographische Klinik von Jean-Martin Charcot*, Munich: Fink, 1997

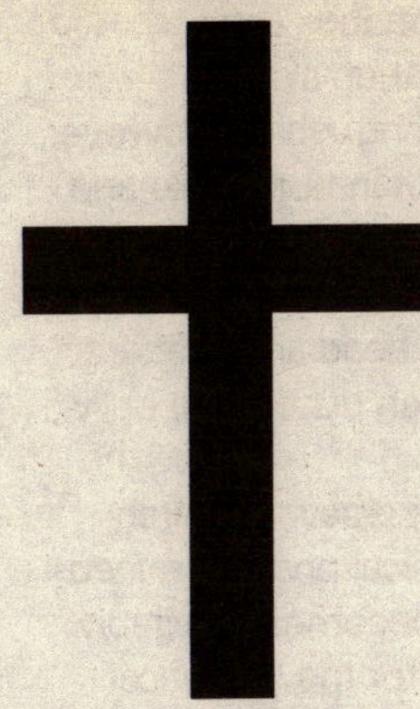

Figure 4

'In these contortions, invariably bizarre, random and
unpredictable positions appear; we have thus also…
described them as illogical positions, among which, however,
one preferred position has been made out in both male and
female patients. We thought the description of 'arched circle'
accurate for this position. In it, the body of the sufferer is
bent completely backwards until only his head and feet are
supporting him on the bed, while his (often distended) belly
forms the point of the arch.'[15] (figure 5)
As Georges Didi-Hubermann argues, Freud saw this arch
primarily as an 'energetic denial of a physical position suited
for sexual intercourse.'[16] Thus, the arch becomes inevitably
identified with sexuality, and, worse yet, for the hysterical,
and therefore diseased, rejection of the same. Loos's position
must be seen in the context of this discourse: the arch of
the curved line signifies for Loos, the degeneration or
dissolution of the sexual into the pathological. Despite all
this, Loos should not be seen as an opponent of the erotic
in general. Beatriz Colomina has convincingly demonstrated
how Loos pursued a clear segregation of public exterior
space and private interior space in his design strategies.
While his facades emphasise the moral and socio-educational
claims of his architecture, in the intimate sphere of the
interior spaces, Loos permits himself the construction of
what are to some extent 'innocent' spaces, in which
a 'natural' and 'healthy' sexuality may reign. According
to Colomina: 'The interior space is, for Loos, a pre oedipal
space, a space predating the analytical distance that resulted
from language, a space that we feel so to speak as a
garment; that is to say as a garment before the appearance
of finished clothing.'[17]

15
Jean-Martin Charcot and Paul Richer, *Die Besessenen in der Kunst*, Göttingen: Steidel,
1988, p 121
16
Ibid, p 295
17
Beatriz Colomina, 'Die gespaltene Wand: Häuslicher Voyeurismus', in, *Privileg Blick Kritik
der visuellen Kultur*, (ed.) Christina Kravagna, Berlin: ID-Archiv, 1997, p 209

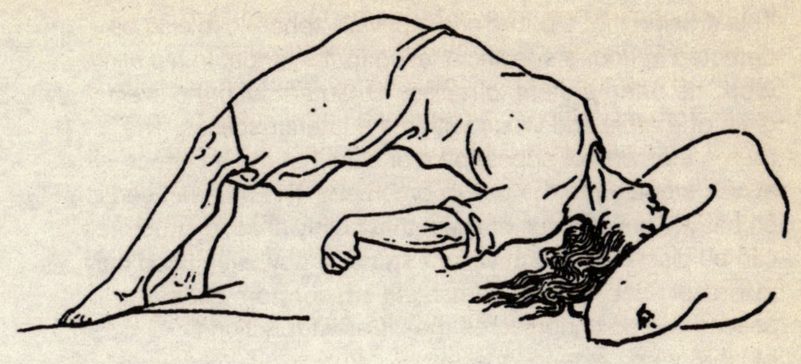

Figure 5
This image is a medical
drawing by an
unknown author which
has been reproduced
from the book by
Jean-Martin Charcot
and Paul Richer,
*Les démoniaques
dans l'art*. Paris, 1887
(Unchanged Reprint
Amsterdam 1972),
p 93

This division into a public and a private sphere can also be detected in Loos's specific relation to the stripe. In his early work, he often prefers to replace ornament with the lively grain of marble and wood within the interior spaces. The rooms thus do not appear bare or cold, but the architect avoids stooping to the use of ornament. The marble used is so heavily grained, full of lines, that nearly chaotic structures can be discerned. Such vibrant stone is, however, used only in interior spaces, or to demarcate interior from exterior spaces and so underscores the different functions of interior and exterior spaces.

Loos's late work shows a retreat from this chaos of lines on columns and wall designs. In his apartment for Willy Kraus in Pilsen, 1930, the stripes now predominate, even in the grain of stone and wood. Loos initially experimented with his strategy of the stripe as a de-eroticised anti-ornament for facades and public spaces. Only later, as part of his educational endeavours against female sensuality, did he apply the strategy to the private sphere.

It would undoubtedly be of interest to follow this cultural history of the stripe in other areas of design. I am particularly struck by the image of tattooed criminals in prison being forced to wear black-and-white striped uniforms – precisely to restore 'discipline and order'.

Notes on the contributors

Monika Aichele is an illustrator who lives and works in New York, Barcelona and Berlin. Her recent commissions include front covers for the *New York Times* Book Review, *New York Times* Arts and Leisure Supplement, *Doubleday*, *Weekend Post* Canada and the *Suedeutsche Zeitung* Magazin

Judith Zaugg is a cartoonist and illustrator who currently lives in Berne. Her publications include *Susa Flott und ihre haarsträubende Geschichte* (Berne: Lucha Libro 2001) and *Bruno Orso fliegt ins Weltall* (Stuttgart: Maroverlag 1997)

Dominique Lämmli is a fine artist, who works with text and computer-based imagery and has exhibited her work in Luzern, Berlin and Saint Etienne

Barry Dainton is a lecturer in Philosophy at the University of Liverpool. He is the author of the book *Time and Space* (Chesham: Acumen 2001)

Ulrike Noack is a fine artist and illustrator who has exhibited her collages in Berlin, Cologne and Leipzig

Slavoj Žižek is a researcher at the Institute of Social Sciences at the University of Ljubljana. His publications include *The Sublime Object of Ideology* (London: Verso 1989), *For they know not what they do* (London: Verso 1991) and *Welcome to the Desert of the Real* (London: Verso 2002)

Christophe Marchand-Kiss is a writer, literary critic and translator into French of the works of Edgar Allan Poe, Herman Melville, John Cage and Yoko Ono. He has also published the novel *L'anthropologue* (Paris: Comp' Act 1995)

Gordon Shrigley is an artist currently living in London and is the author of the book *Insignificance, A short Discourse on the Physical and Ideational Economy of Line within Architectural representation* (Stuttgart: Solitude Editions 1998)

Sarah Treadwell is a practicing architect and is professor of Architecture at the University of Auckland, New Zealand. Her essays have appeared in *Fabrications, Form/Work, Space & Culture,* and *Interstices: Journal of Architecture and Related Arts*

Annette Geiger is an art historian currently teaching as assistant professor of Art and Design History at the University of Art, Berlin. Her book on the artist Chardin is forthcoming from the German publishers Fink

Daniel Welton is a graphic designer and founder member of eight design, London. He is also a visiting lecturer in Typography at West Hertfordshire College

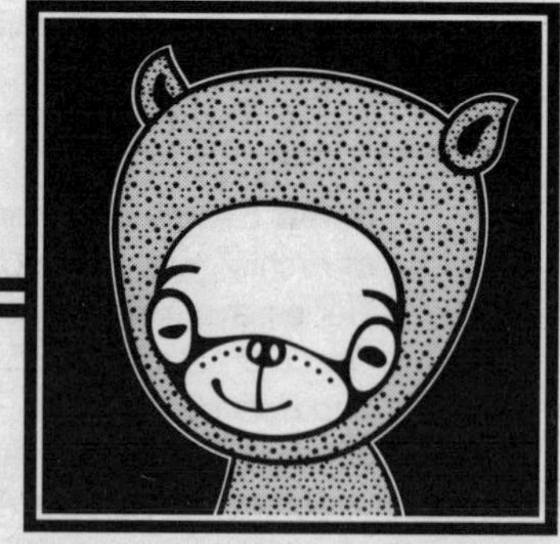